KICKBOXING FOR WOMEN

by Jennifer Lawler & Debz Buller

Wish Publishing
Terre Haute, Indiana
www.wishpublishing.com

Kickboxing for Women © 2002 Jennifer Lawler and Debz Buller

LCCN: 2001093666

The author and the publisher assume no responsibility for any injury that may occur as a result of attempting to do any of the movements, techniques or exercises described in this book. These activities require strenuous physical activity and a physical examination is advisable before starting this or any other exercise activity.

Proofread by Heather Lowhorn
Cover designed by Phil Velikan
Cover photo by Mark Cass, PictureQuest
Interior photography by Jennifer Lawler

Printed in the United States of America
10 9 8 7 6 5 4 3 2 1

Published in the United States by
Wish Publishing
P.O. Box 10337
Terre Haute, IN 47801, USA
www.wishpublishing.com

Distributed in the United States by
Cardinal Publishers Group
7301 Georgetown Road, Suite 118
Indianapolis, Indiana 46268
www.cardinalpub.com

*Jennifer would like to dedicate this book to her daughter Jessica,
a living lesson in perseverance.*

*Debz would like to dedicate this book to her mother, Wayne Ann,
who personified the ultimate warrior spirit alive in all women.*

The authors would like to express their appreciation to Gold's Gym and Ringside in Merriam, Kansas, and Sixth Street Fitness in Lawrence, Kansas, for their permission to shoot photos on-site. We also appreciate Rod Keiser of The Dragon's Choice for supplying the workout gear, and Top Ten, the maker of said workout gear. Finally, special thanks goes to the people who appear in the photos: Chantal Anderson; Kay Traver, Ronnie Williams, Jr.; Scott A. Hallock, Jr. and Dave Buller.

TABLE OF CONTENTS

INTRODUCTION

Each year, thousands of people begin kickboxing. Surprisingly, the majority of these people are women. It's a great time for this sport, reflected in the number of women (of all ages, but particularly younger women) who show up for training classes at gyms throughout the country. With virtually every popular woman's character in movies and television shows exhibiting some sort of kickboxing or martial arts prowess, the trend will probably continue for some time.

Thousands more women join related classes, such as aerobox, cardio-kickboxing, Tae Bo and the like. Once these women start learning some of the techniques of kickboxing, they often want to learn more. And once they have learned the basics of kickboxing, many want to fight professionally, but don't know where to find a coach or how to prepare for full-contact competition. This book is for all of these women.

Whether you attempt to learn on your own or through classes offered by experienced instructors, you may eventually feel the need to have a skills book to help you with your practice. Most women, however, must purchase books intended for men, since little kickboxing information is directed toward a female audience. While you can, of course, benefit from material written for men, you may find it more useful to have information written with you in mind. Some of the challenges that women in sports face are not faced by men, and many of the inherent skills that many women have (speed, agility) are often overlooked in traditional reference books.

Kickboxing for Women corrects that problem. It covers all the essentials of learning kickboxing, plus tips especially for women. It contains information helpful to beginner, intermediate, and advanced kickboxers. *Kickboxing for Women* covers principles, techniques and drills for the fitness kickboxer as well as the professional kickboxer. Debz Buller, a kickboxing instructor, provides quotes and training ideas. Numerous photographs illustrate the techniques so that you can practice them. A resource directory helps you find equipment, supplies and other like-minded kickboxers.

The authors, Jennifer Lawler and Debz Buller have extensive experience in martial arts and combat sports. Jennifer Lawler, a second-degree black belt in Tae Kwon Do, has experience in Aikido, Combat Hapkido, Karate, Hapkido, Aiki-jutsu and the weapons of self-defense. She has been a tournament competitor for almost 10 years and a tournament judge since 1994. She is the author of more than a dozen books. Many of her books are about the martial arts, including *Tae Kwon Do for Women, Martial Arts for Women: A Practical Guide, Secrets of Tae Kwon Do, Coaching Women in the Martial Arts, The Martial Arts Encyclopedia* and *Freestyle Sparring* (with Grandmaster Woo Jin Jung). Her forthcoming titles from Wish Publishing include *Punch! Why Women Participate in Violent Sports* and *The Encyclopedia of Girls' and Women's Sports.*

Lawler has written for a number of magazines, including the *Black Book, Karate/Kung-Fu Illustrated, Weight Watchers, Women's Circle* and *Martial Arts and Combat Sports*. She earned her Ph.D. in English from the University of Kansas in 1996. She is a member of the American Black Belt Association, the International Tae Kwon Do Federation, the National Women's Martial Arts Federation and the Association of Women Martial Arts Instructors.

Debz Buller, a certified Cardio-Karate teacher (National Association of Professional Martial Artists), ACE aerobics instructor and ISSA certified personal trainer, has taught a wide variety of kickboxing and aerobic kickboxing classes, including her popular SHRED program, at martial arts schools and gyms throughout the country. She is a silver medalist in Kali (Filipino stickfighting) and Panantukan (Filipino kickboxing) and is a member of the U.S. National Kali Team. She is also a member of the World Escrima, Kali and Arnis Federation.

Buller brings her experience as a kickboxer, competitor and teacher to the book. She has spent the last several years studying with some of the world's greatest martial arts masters and has ranking and experience in Ki-Aikido, Tae Kwon Do, Muay Thai Kickboxing, Oyama Karate, Chen-style Tai Chi/Gung Fu, Jun Fan Jeet Kun Do and possesses a black belt in self-defense from the American Self Defense Association. In addition, her studies with other masters have allowed her to develop keen streetfighting, weapons, combat and self-defense applications from Australia, South America, Israel, Indonesia, Russia, South Africa and the Orient.

She spends a great deal of time continuing her martial arts/self-defense education and sharing her knowledge and experience through teaching, writing, lecturing and demonstrations. Her main focus at present is in providing practical self-defense education to the general public and in assisting women in their pursuit of achievement through competition.

We hope that this book will help you succeed as a kickboxer and reach all of your kickboxing goals.

Jennifer Lawler and Debz Buller
Lawrence, Kansas
December 1, 2001

1

INTRODUCTION TO KICKBOXING

Kickboxing, a hybrid sport, combines techniques used in American boxing, Karate, Thai boxing and Tae Kwon Do. Although kickboxing is not considered a traditional martial art like Aikido or Judo—instead, it is thought of as a sport and is sometimes called a combat sport—its beginnings extend far back in time.

In classical Greece, athletes fought each other using boxing and wrestling techniques in a sport called Pancration. This sport included grappling, hitting, kicking and throwing. Although it may have resembled kickboxing, it is not the direct ancestor of the sport. Instead, Pancration influenced other sports (and martial arts) and these other sports form the back bone of kickboxing.

Thai kickboxing, also called Muay Thai, began in what is now Thailand. Its origins are unclear, but it may have come from China, which had martial artists called "boxers" who performed traditional martial arts techniques such as hand strikes, throws, and kicks. Muay Thai is considerably more brutal than the kickboxing performed in other parts of the world, and the average career of a Muay Thai kickboxer is less than five years.

Another form of kickboxing, Savate, developed in France during the 17th century. The techniques were probably learned in Asian countries by French sailors, then brought back to France, where they were used in street fights. At first, these fighters simply used kicks to defend themselves (or perhaps to attack other people) but over time American boxing techniques were added. By the 19th century, Savate had become a popular form of self-defense, especially among the upper classes, who enjoyed watching Savate competitions.

Modern Karate, which was developed in the 20th century by Funakoshi Gichin, teaches the use of both the "empty" hand and weapons (especially weapons fashioned from farming implements, what might be called "environmental" weapons). Karate developed on the island of

1

Okinawa, where martial arts had been brought by Chinese settlers. Funakoshi helped spread Karate from Okinawa to Japan and eventually throughout the world. Many different styles of Karate exist, but all styles rely on hand and leg strikes and blocks.

Tae Kwon Do, which used to be called "Korean Karate," is a system of fighting that emphasizes kicks. Based on traditional Korean martial arts and influenced by Japanese martial arts, modern Tae Kwon Do was organized and systematized by General Choi after World War II. It has become one of the most popular martial arts in the world.

All of these martial arts and combat sports influenced the development of modern kickboxing. Unlike other martial arts, modern kickboxing does not have a system of philosophy; nor is it considered a "way," the traditional designation given to martial arts that provide a blueprint for living in a balanced, harmonious life. Kickboxing is a sport, and it is taught as such. This does not mean that people who kickbox don't, won't or can't devote time and energy to cultivating such a balanced, harmonious life, just that this is not the emphasis of the sport.

In 1974, the Professional Kickboxers Association was established to promote the sport and to ensure that fighters were kept safer by insisting on the use of padded equipment. It also standardized the guidelines for matches. For example, it set a minimum number of kicks each fighter must perform during each round (eight kicks above the waist). It also determined that a match consisted of 12 two-minute rounds with a one minute rest between.

There are many different kinds of kickboxing and aerobic kickboxing taught and practiced throughout the world. In other countries, such as Japan and Russia, kickboxing techniques are combined with other martial arts techniques, such as throws, to create new hybrid sports like shootboxing. In Thai kickboxing, fighters are allowed to use techniques, such as elbow strikes, that are not allowed in other forms of kickboxing because of how dangerous these techniques are.

In the United States, women can take up kickboxing training with an eye toward becoming a professional or just to get in shape. They can also participate in aerobic kickboxing classes, which teach some of the basic techniques but don't allow students to spar each other. These classes go by names such as Tae-Bo, cardio-kickboxing and aerobox. It is important to realize that aerobic kickboxing does not provide participants with real world self-defense skills. Only regular kickboxing training with an experienced coach can provide this.

FOR WOMEN ONLY: Many women are most comfortable starting with aerobic kickboxing before committing to more serious, intense training. Once they have practiced some of the basic techniques in this non-contact form of kickboxing, many are ready to move onto more hardcore training, where they will spar with partners and perhaps enter tournament competitions.

DEBZ SAYS: Kickboxing classes range in style, difficulty and contact, from the true aerobics class to endurance training for professional bouts. I am a fanatic about making it clear that most cardio or aerobic kickboxing classes do NOT provide enough information or proper practice to defend oneself in an attack. Make sure you know what you're getting into when you sign up!

2
BENEFITS OF KICKBOXING TRAINING

You don't have to compete in professional matches in order to enjoy the benefits of kickboxing, but you do have to train as if you were. If you train half-heartedly or show up for class only on alternate Tuesdays, you won't reap the benefits of training in kickboxing. And the benefits are very real. While you might expect physical results, you will also feel mental and emotional rewards as well.

If you practice kickboxing regularly, you can lose weight and become stronger. Your legs grow stronger from the kicks; your upper body grows stronger from the punches. You will gain greater endurance since much of your training will consist of continuous repetition of techniques. Over time, you will notice that your daily activities have become easier and that you have more stamina.

A kickboxing workout is both aerobic and anaerobic, so your cardiovascular system benefits just as your ability to sprint (or otherwise work hard) for short periods will also improve. This means you aren't neglecting any important aspect of staying in shape.

Kickboxing also helps you increase flexibility and agility. In order to perform the moves, you have to be able to kick high, twist and move around. You may not be able to kick high right at first, but with practice, you will develop this skill. Your balance will improve (because kicking requires that you stand on one leg only while performing the kick). Your reactions will become faster as you look for openings when you spar. All of these physical benefits extend into your daily life as well, making you feel more fit and alert even when you're sitting at your desk at work. And if you have to run to catch the bus, you won't be out of breath like everyone else is!

A typical kickboxing workout can burn twice as many calories as a traditional aerobics class, so training in kickboxing can help you lose weight or maintain an optimum weight. It increases your energy, builds stronger bones and muscles and makes you feel more powerful.

The benefits of kickboxing aren't just physical, though. As you train, you will notice that intense physical exertion helps relieve stress. Because you must focus on your physical performance, you can forget what a bad day you had at the office or how much the kids whined. Because you have to focus on your physical performance, you learn mental discipline to keep from getting distracted (getting distracted in the ring will earn you bumps and bruises, not to mention causing you to lose the match). Learning to focus despite distractions allows you to develop improved powers of concentration that can overlap into your everyday life.

Training also improves your self-esteem. As your body gets into better shape, you feel better about it. As you train in the techniques of kickboxing and learn what your body can do, you begin to have a better body image and more self-confidence. Training in kickboxing also makes you feel more confident that you could protect yourself in a fight, so you become less afraid of muggers and rapists and more in control of your life. These feelings of empowerment may prove to be more important to you than any physical benefits you receive.

If you train in aerobic kickboxing only, you will receive many of the same physical and mental benefits—improved fitness, stress relief—but you should realize that the techniques you learn in an aerobic kickboxing class should not be relied on for self-defense. Often, these instructors are simply aerobics teachers. Some of them have a few hours of training in kickboxing or martial arts techniques. Since you never spar with others in mock combat, you don't get a chance to "use" your techniques to understand how they work against another person (as opposed to just a heavy bag). So while aerobic kickboxing classes can be worthwhile, they are not the same thing as training in kickboxing.

By committing yourself to training in kickboxing, you will begin to notice changes almost immediately. Your muscle tone becomes firmer; you feel less stressed; you focus more completely on your goals. These benefits continue to build and expand as you continue to train and acquire new and useful kickboxing skills.

FOR WOMEN ONLY: If you're thinking of taking up kickboxing in order to learn self-defense techniques, make sure you train with an experienced kickboxer and that you spar with male and female partners. Otherwise, you may not be able to use the techniques, or you may not use them correctly, if you are ever confronted by an attacker.

FOR WOMEN ONLY: Kickboxing relies on technique for effectiveness. This means a skilled woman can defeat a bigger, stronger man if she has superior technique. Don't discount the fact that you can protect yourself even from people who are much bigger than you are. You just have to practice your techniques correctly.

DEBZ SAYS: Anyone can benefit from training in kickboxing. I've had students ranging in age from 18 to 57! As always, check with your doctor before starting any training program. If you happen to be a young girl, you can also benefit from training in kickboxing, but I don't recommend contact kickboxing until you reach age 18 (at least!).

3
WHERE TO BEGIN

Once you're ready to begin kickboxing, you need to find a place to train, and you need to purchase appropriate work out clothes and equipment.

The most important of these is finding the right place to train. This means finding the right coach or instructor, and that's easier said than done. You don't want to get hurt or discouraged, so you must have competent instruction. Some martial artists, accomplished in a martial art like Tae Kwon Do or Karate, assume they can teach kickboxing, too. Although martial arts experience is helpful, actual kickboxing experience is more important. However, being a world champion at one time or another does not guarantee that a coach will be any good. Some of the best teachers—and this is true of all sports—were never superstars themselves.

So how do you find the right coach? First, ask around at area gyms to see which offer kickboxing instruction. You may also find individuals listed as kickboxing instructors in the phone directory or on Internet websites. When you investigate gym-based kickboxing programs, find out who the instructors are (if there is more than one) and what their qualifications are. Find out what classes are available and how instruction is offered (small class, large class, one-on-one), and be certain you understand how much it is going to cost to train.

Watch a couple of training sessions before you sign up. Notice how the instructor interacts with the students. Does he or she encourage them and demonstrate proper technique, or does he or she just bark out commands? When the students spar, do they demonstrate control, or do they just whack away at each other?

The training room itself should be large enough that students don't run into each other while practicing techniques. The floor should be cushioned with wood flooring or carpeting (not tile or concrete). Mirrors should line the walls so that you can see what you're doing. There should be equipment like heavy bags and focus mitts for you to use.

If you're just interested in aerobic kickboxing, the only equipment you will need is comfortable clothing (loose shorts and T-shirts). If you will be using a heavy bag in the class, you may need bag gloves or hand wraps (the instructor can tell you ahead of time).

If you're training in actual, no-holds-barred kickboxing, though, you will need to invest in safety equipment. Not only does safety equipment protect you, it protects your training partners. Purchase good brands that will hold up well to wear and tear (new is preferable to used).

You will need hand wraps, bag gloves, boxing gloves, headgear, mouthguard, chest protector and foot and shin guards. You may also want to purchase special shoes to protect your feet while you're kicking the heavy bag. Martial arts shoes and wrestling shoes are good choices for this. You can expect to spend several hundred dollars getting outfitted for training. Handwraps cost about $10, bag gloves about $50, boxing gloves run $50-$150, mouthguards $5 (custom dental mouthguards run more like $100), chest protectors cost about $30-$50, foot and shin guards cost about $30, and headgear runs between $75-$150. Protective shoes run between $50 and $75. This totals $300 at the low end and more than $600 at the high end, including shoes. It can be a very good idea to invest in equipment incrementally. For instance, as a beginner you may just need handwraps and bag gloves. As you continue to train (and by the time you actually spar with partners), you can progress to investing in safety equipment such as a mouthguard and headgear. This approach ensures that you know you like kickboxing before you drop two weeks' pay on equipment that will gather dust in the closest.

If you train frequently, your equipment may need to be replaced every year. If you workout only once or twice a week, your equipment may last two or three years. As soon as you see cracks or tears in the material, it's time for new equipment. Once your handwraps lose their elasticity, it's time for new handwraps.

You can purchase most of your needs from a sporting goods store. Many cities have martial arts stores that can provide you with your equipment. In addition, your gym may have a pro shop where you can purchase the items you need. If all else fails, mail order merchants, included in the resource directory at the back of the book, can help you out.

Handwraps protect your hands, especially your knuckles, from the effects of repeated punching. Different types of material are used in handwraps. The easiest material to use resembles an elastic bandage. This is easier to wrap around your hands and the elastic compresses your hand slightly to give good support. Your trainer can help you wrap your hands (see figure 1), but it helps to be self-sufficient and learn to

wrap your own hands. To use this type of handwrap, slip the thumb loop over your thumb. Then pull the wrap over the back of your hand. Wrap around your wrist two or three times. Cross the wrap under your hand and wrap the back of your hand, covering your knuckles, two or three times. Slant the wrap back down to your thumb and wrap the thumb. Then, wrap around the wrist and knuckles again. Secure the

1

wrap. (See figures 2 - 9.) This wrap is sufficient for beginners. For advanced kickboxers, you will want to wrap through your fingers. Follow the instructions for the previous wrap. After you have covered your knuckles (figure 7), instead of working your way down to your thumb,

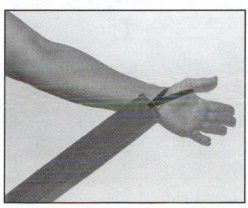

2

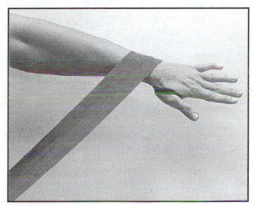

3

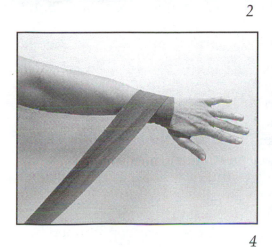

4

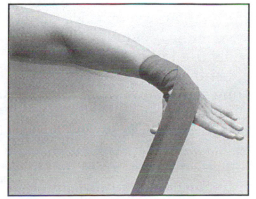

5

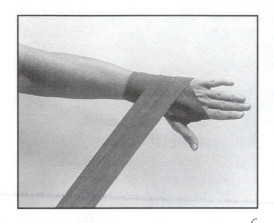

6

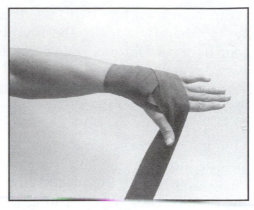

7

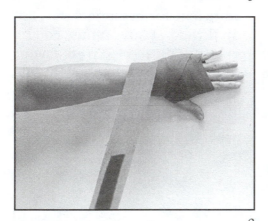

8

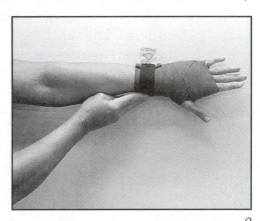

9

guide the wrap between your ring finger and pinky finger, pulling the wrap down tightly. Then wrap each finger individually, weaving the wrap through your fingers. Cross the wrap over the back of your hand. Then wrap your wrist once or twice and secure the wrap. You can start the wrap over your little finger (see figures 10–16) or you can start the wrap under your little finger (see figures 17–21 on page 12). Your personal comfort will dictate your choice.

With either handwrap, make certain you do not pull the wrap too snug or you can cut off the circulation in your hands.

Bag gloves, which are worn when you spar the heavy bag, have special padding around the knuckles to protect them. Make sure to try on bag gloves before you purchase them. Lighter weight gloves (five or six ounces) offer less protection than heavier gloves (12 ounces) but don't tire your arms as much. Beginners should invest in heavier weight gloves for the added protection. Once your hands are more conditioned and you have practiced your techniques repeatedly (and therefore make fewer

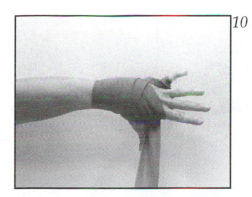
10

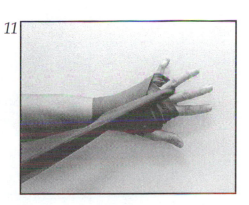
11

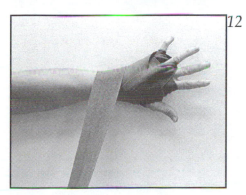
12

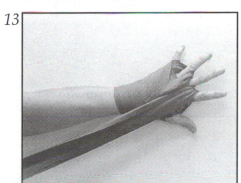
13

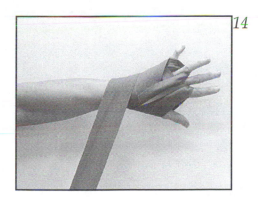
14

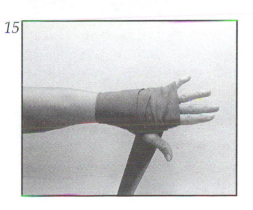
15

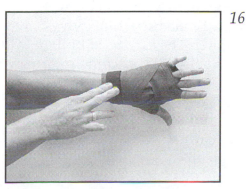
16

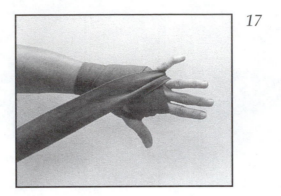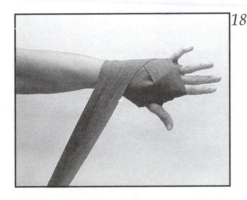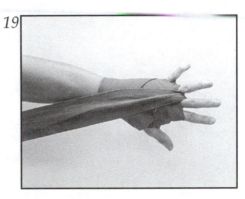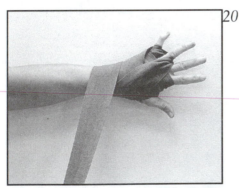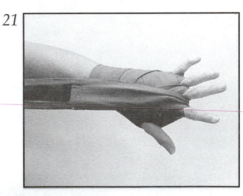

mistakes), you can move up to the lighter weight gloves.

Boxing gloves, also called sparring gloves, are used when you actually fight another fighter. They are used both in training sessions and in formal competition. Boxing gloves come in three weights: 14 ounce, 16 ounce and 18 ounce. Most fighters use the 16 ounce, while heavyweight and hardhitting kickboxers use the 18 ounce. Women may prefer the 14 ounce since it is more suitable for their size. In addition to weight, gloves come in different sizes (thus, you can have a large 14 ounce glove and a small 18 ounce glove). Sizes are usually small, medium, large and extra large.

Simple mouthguards can be purchased inexpensively and will save you from ruinous dental bills. The kind you buy at a sporting goods store should suffice for most of your needs. If you plan to kickbox professionally, however, it is in your best interest to purchase a custom dental mouthguard. The typical storebought mouthguard can be molded to fit your upper row of teeth. Pop it in boiling water, slip it in your mouth and bite down. It will conform to your bite. If it's too large, you can shape it with a pair of sharp scissors. Another type, the double-layered mouthpiece, protects both upper and lower rows of teeth and is not much more expensive than the single layer type. It can be formed to fit the same way. A custom-made mouthguard must be purchased from a dentist who will build it to fit your mouth exactly. It is important that no matter which type you use, the mouthguard should not interfere with your breathing. Keep trying until you find one that works for you.

Investing in good headgear is essential. This helps protect your brain from blows to your head. You don't want to end up with boxer's dementia just because you were determined to lose a few extra pounds. Your headgear should be designed for sparring and training in kickboxing. It will help prevent damage such as cuts and bruises and also help protect from longer term damage that can result from getting your bell rung regularly. Make certain your headgear fits correctly. It shouldn't be so tight that you get a headache when you're wearing it; nor should it be so loose that it spins around your head when you sweat.

Women rarely wear groin protectors, although there are some on the market designed just for women. A chest protector is mandatory for women who kickbox professionally. Even if you're just sparring in training, it can be a worthwhile investment. You don't need a bulky protector that covers you from neck to thigh like you see some martial artists wear. A kickboxing chest protector is small and made of molded plastic. It fits inside your sports bra.

Shin and foot guards protect your shins and feet from bumps and bruises. Most women swear by them. The first time someone's elbow smashes into your shin, you will also swear by them. Look for a one piece padded protector that covers the entire shin and instep of your foot. If you don't purchase one that covers your instep, you may need to buy a separate foot protector. This covers the top and sides of your feet, leaving the soles of your feet uncovered.

You may not use all of this equipment all of the time, but it is worthwhile to have it on hand. In addition to safety equipment, you should invest in comfortable workout clothes, such as shorts and a T-shirt. Some women train in their sports bras and shorts, while others are not comfortable with this approach and prefer to cover up more. If you do wear a shirt, always tuck it into your shorts so that loose clothing does not catch on someone's foot. Never wear jewelry (not even your wedding ring) when you're working out. This is dangerous for you and your sparring partners. Also, wash off the makeup (it can run, get in your eyes and smear on your clothes) and keep your hair cut short or pulled back from your face.

If you want to create a home gym so that you can train at home in your spare time, you will have to invest an additional several hundred dollars. You will still need professional instruction, so that you know how to perform the techniques correctly but if your lifestyle or schedule forces you to do much of your training at home, you can still make progress as a kickboxer.

To get started, you will need a clear space. An area that's about 8 x 8 is ideal, but if you don't have this much room to spare, you can still work out at home. You may not be able to store and use as much equipment, but it may still be worth the effort.

Choose an area that has a cushioned floor (wood or carpeted). The garage is not the best choice, since bouncing around on the concrete can be very hard on your joints, not to mention your bones. You should outfit your workout space with mirrors, since you need to see your body to make certain you're performing techniques correctly. If you have access to a video camera, you can have someone record your workout and then you can review and critique your performance. This can be especially helpful if you're planning to become a professional.

You can also invest in some or all of the following, in descending order of importance:

♦ *Heavy bag.* Kicking and punching the heavy bag builds muscle and skill. Some heavy bags are hung from a ceiling joist (these are the most popular). Freestanding heavy bags are more suitable for people who don't have a handy ceiling joist, or who rent and do not want to explain to their landlord why that huge screw is jutting out of the ceiling tiles. Freestanding heavy bags are filled with water and can be adjusted to suit your height. Some freestanding heavy bags are shaped to resemble a person with target areas clearly marked. A special kickboxing bag, which is 7–8 feet long, is designed to help you practice sweeps and low kicks. Bags come in vinyl, canvas and leather. Although the canvas kind looks authentic, it can tear up your equipment, so vinyl is a better choice. A good heavy bag will run about $100–$150.

♦ *Jump rope.* The lowly jump rope is an excellent training aid. Jumping rope improves your physical condition and your timing. These come in various weights; the heavier ones, of course, being harder to swing, improve your physical endurance faster than lighter weight ropes do. Make sure you get one in the right length. A good jump rope costs about $15.

♦ *Focus mitts.* These are pads slightly larger than a sheet of paper (and of course much thicker). Your partner or trainer moves the mitt around as you perform a series of techniques and attempt to strike it. These cost $30–$60.

♦ *Thai pads.* These thick pads are rectangles measuring about 10 inches wide and 20 inches long. A partner holds straps that are sewn to the back of the pad. Like the focus mitt, the partner moves this pad around as you kick from different angles. These cost $50–$75.

♦ *Kicking pad.* These are heavy pads about twice as large as Thai pads that allow you to kick full force without worrying about hurting your training partner. These cost about $50.

♦ *Speed bag.* The speed bag is about the size of a basketball. It attaches to wall or ceiling, and it moves around as you strike it with your hands. Working the speed bag correctly requires excellent timing. These cost between $30–$50.

♦ *Double-end bag.* The double-end bag is attached at both ends. As you strike it, it bounces around. Instead of developing a rhythm as you strike (which you do with the speed bag), you simply have to react to the double-end bag since you cannot predict its movement. This reaction training can improve your sparring skills. These cost about $50.

♦ *Medicine ball.* This is a weighted ball, of varying sizes and weights (from about 9 to 18 pounds). Throwing this around builds arm strength and abdominal strength. Different exercises force you to bend, twist, curl and otherwise work while throwing the ball to a partner. These run between $30–$50.

Of course, you don't need to set up a complete home gym in order to train at home. In fact, you can train for kickboxing at home just by skipping rope or running. These activities help you get in good physical condition, which will improve your kickboxing performance.

Once you have your clothing and safety equipment, you're ready to begin training. But you may not be sure what's expected of you. It's hard to generalize, because there are many types of kickboxing workouts available—non-contact classes, aerobic kickboxing, one-on-one training sessions, and regular kickboxing classes where you work with other students. This is why it's important to ask questions before you hand over your hard-earned cash, so that you have a clear idea of what you're getting into.

At the start of each workout, you should spend some time warming up and stretching, then do the workout, then cool down with additional stretches. During each workout session, you should do body conditioning exercises, repetition of kicking and punching techniques, bag work (heavy bag, focus mitts, speed bag and the like) and, depending on your training, a sparring session.

Just remember that as a beginner, you have every right to express discomfort with what you're being asked to do. Therefore, if you're really not ready to jump in the ring and spar, then don't. Keep in mind, though, that a good instructor may encourage you to do something before you're certain you're ready because some people, left to their own devices, would never be ready. It's part of your coach's job to encourage you to achieve more than you thought possible. Therefore, it's important that you can trust your coach to help you make the right decisions about your skill level and abilities.

FOR WOMEN ONLY: Some headgear comes with face protectors, either made of plastic or of a plastic "cage." This can be a smart investment if you don't want to sport a broken nose and two black eyes on your next hot date.

FOR WOMEN ONLY: Some manufacturers are now making bag and boxing gloves sized specifically for women, who have smaller hands than men. Consider investing in these especially designed gloves rather than just settling for a small size of men's gloves.

DEBZ SAYS: Try before you buy. Make sure the clothing and equipment you purchase work for you. Boxing gloves that are too heavy just discourage you from punching; headgear that blocks your peripheral vision can be dangerous! Ask your instructor how your equipment should fit and get his or her recommendation for where to buy your kickboxing supplies. Once you're outfitted, get your coach's approval on your "look": he or she may be able to tell you that you've got your shin guards on backward. It's better to know that *before* you step into the ring.

4
WARM-UPS AND STRETCHES

Before working out in any sport, it's important to warm up and stretch your muscles in order to avoid injury and to improve performance. And it's just as important to stretch and cool down *after* a workout. By warming up your muscles, you will be less likely to strain and stress them. You'll also prepare your joints for vigorous activity. By stretching, you increase your flexibility. Warm up before you stretch by walking briskly, swinging your arms, jogging slowly, jumping rope lightly, climbing stairs, or otherwise gently putting your muscles in motion. Your warm up should last 5–10 minutes. You should begin to feel warmer and have a light sweat before beginning your stretches.

Stretches must be done correctly to benefit you. Overstretching or stretching incorrectly can actually cause injury, so be careful to slowly stretch into the stretch position, hold the stretch for at least 15 seconds, continuing to breath slowly as you stretch. Don't bounce. If the stretch hurts, stop immediately. The suggested stretches here should be done both before and after a kickboxing training session. As you gain more experience, you may wish to add more and different stretches. Just remember to stretch every major muscle group. It helps to work from the neck down so that you don't overlook a muscle group.

Neck stretch

Stretch your neck in each of the four directions. First, tilt your head down and tuck your chin toward your chest. Hold the stretch for 15 seconds. Next, tilt your head back so that you're staring at the ceiling. Hold for 15 seconds. Next, tilt your

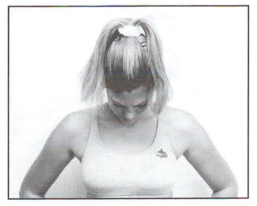

22

head to the left, as if you're trying to touch your ear to your shoulder. Keep your shoulders relaxed as you do this. Hold for 15 seconds. Next, tilt your head to the right, as if you're trying to touch your ear to your shoulder. Keep your shoulders relaxed. Hold for 15 seconds. Repeat all four stretches. Don't roll your head since this can pinch a nerve. Instead, do simple stretches in each direction. (See figure 22.)

Advanced neck stretch

For a more advanced neck stretch, use your hand to apply light pressure as you move your ear to your shoulder. You may also opt to use a towel as a sling, lightly pulling the ends forward as you resist backward with the head. Place the towel/sling around your forehead and reverse the stretch by resisting forward with your head. (See figures 23–25).

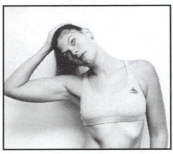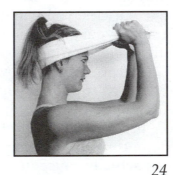

23   24   25

Shoulder stretch

With your arm straight, reach toward your opposite shoulder without turning your body. Using your opposite hand to push against your

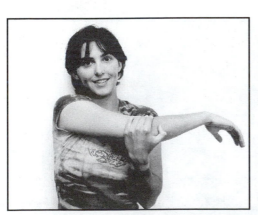

elbow. You should feel this stretch in the back of your shoulder. Hold for fifteen seconds. Repeat the technique with your opposite arm. (See figure 26.)

Advanced shoulder stretch

For a deeper, more advanced stretch, turn your head and look past the shoulder being stretched. Point your arm downward at a 45-degree angle to lengthen the stretch. (See figure 27.)

26

27   28

Variation: Instead of reaching over your opposite shoulder, reach over your head, again using your opposite arm to push against your elbow. You should feel the stretch under your arm. Hold for 15 seconds and repeat with opposite arm (See figure 28.)

Shoulder shrug

Lift your shoulders up toward your ears. Hold the position for 15 seconds. Lower your shoulders, relax and repeat. Remember to completely relax your neck and jaw at all times. (See figures 29–30).

29   30

Back stretch

Sit on the floor with your legs directly out in front of you. Inhale deeply, reaching upward, then slowly exhale as you bend forward trying to touch your hands to the soles of your feet. Hold the position for 15 seconds. Relax and repeat. (See figure 31.)

31

32

33

34

Variation: If this stretch puts stress on your knees, bend your legs so that the soles of your feet touch each other, then lean forward and stretch, holding the position for 15 seconds. (See figure 32.)

Hip stretch

Kneel on the floor. Bend one knee so that the sole of your foot touches the floor. Roll your hips forward until you feel the stretch in your hip. Make sure you do not bend your knee too far forward. It should never angle past your foot; instead, the bend should stay at about 90 degrees. Hold the position for 15 seconds, then switch legs and repeat. (See figure 33.)

Thigh stretch

Lying on your stomach, hands under your head for support, lift one leg as far as possible off the ground. Hold the position for 15 seconds, then repeat on the other leg. (See figure 34.)

35

36

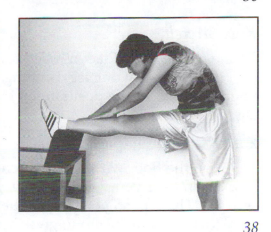

37

38

Hamstring stretch

Lie with your back on the floor. Place a rolled towel in the small of your back to support your back if necessary. Lift one leg toward your shoulder. Use your hands to pull your leg closer to your body. If you don't have the flexibility for this, put a towel behind your leg, like a sling, and pull on the towel to ease your leg toward your chest. You should feel the stretch on the back of your leg. Hold the position for 15 seconds. Repeat with the other leg. (See figures 35–37.)

Alternative: If a barre (a wood railing attached to the wall at chest height) is available, rest your heel against the barre and lean toward your knee. You should feel the stretch in the back of your leg. Hold the position for 15 seconds, then switch legs and repeat. If a barre is unavailable, you may use a wall close to a door frame, the back of a chair, or parts of the many weight machines found in gyms for support. (See figure 38.)

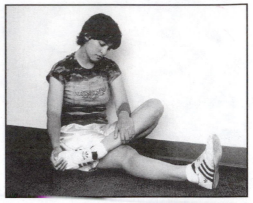

39   40

Knee stretch

Lie on the floor. Place a rolled towel under your lower back for support if needed. Lift one leg, bending at the knee. Pull your knee toward your chest. Hold the position for 15 seconds, then repeat on the other leg. (See figure 39.)

Ankle stretch

Sit on the floor with your legs crossed. Using your hands, pull your foot down as if you were pointing your toes. Hold the position for 15 seconds. Then, push your foot in the opposite direction. Bend your toes back toward your instep to give them a good stretch. This is assists in proper toe placement when executing certain kicks, such as the front kick. Hold the position for 15 seconds. Then stretch your foot in each of the two other directions, holding each stretch for 15 seconds. (See figure 40.)

FOR WOMEN ONLY: Women injure their knees and hips more than men do. Since kickboxing can be hard on these joints, it is important to warm up and stretch before every workout. Avoid exercises that put excessive stress on your knees, such as deep knee bends. Turn to Chapter 13, which discusses weight training, for more information on building up your quadriceps to help strengthen your knees. Make sure you perform the kickboxing techniques correctly in order to avoid putting too much stress on your hips and knees. If you've had knee trouble in the past, your doctor may recommend a stabilizing knee brace so that you can participate in kickboxing. (You may not be allowed to wear this in competition, depending on what type you have, but it can be used during practice.)

DEBZ SAYS: It's important to always keep your spine as straight and elongated as possible by tucking your chin into your chest and tilting your pelvis forward and upward. Calm, even and deep breathing is essential for proper stretching and optimum health. At the beginning of each stretch, inhale as deeply as possible, exhaling slowly and completely during the exertion phase of the stretch. This ensures increased blood/oxygen supplies and decreases the build up of toxic waste products (which cause post-exercise soreness).

5
KICKS

Once you've warmed up and stretched, you're ready to learn and practice the techniques used in kickboxing. Learning to do these techniques doesn't take that long, but mastering them can take months. You'll repeat each technique many times during the course of a training session in order to build "muscle memory" so that you'll be able to perform the techniques without thinking about them. Your body will simply take over.

It is important to practice each technique correctly. Your aim is to execute your kicks, punches and sweeps as perfectly as possible. If you perform the techniques incorrectly, you risk injuring yourself as you train. A poorly-done kick, for example, can over-stress your knees, hamstrings or hips. A correctly done technique is less stressful on your body. Also, a well-executed technique will strike to the target area with power. An incorrectly executed technique may not land where you intend, and you may hit your opponent with more power or with less power than necessary.

Remember that your trainer will have his or her preferences for how you perform the techniques. Your trainer's advice always takes precedence over anything you read in a book! In the following chapter, we describe how to "chamber" and "re-chamber" your kicks. Some trainers feel that unchambered kicks are faster and therefore better for using in the ring. If this is your trainer's perspective, then follow his or her guidelines.

The first techniques you learn are the basic stance position and all of the kicks. The stance is the position you keep your feet and body in as you prepare to fight or to perform the techniques. Kickboxing uses one basic stance, the neutral fighter's stance. It is important to focus on your body position in this stance. Being in the correct stance can help you guard your body from the opponent's strikes. It will also help you keep your balance as you kick and punch. If you're in a poor stance, your opponent could easily knock you down, or you might be unable to perform your kicks as quickly as possible. A poor stance also telegraphs your next move to your partner or opponent. For instance, if you shift all your weight to your back leg in your stance, your partner will know you're getting ready to kick with your front leg and will be prepared to defend against it.

The neutral fighter's stance balances your weight evenly. Both legs bear about 50 percent of your weight. This means your partner will not be able to tell which leg you intend to kick with.

Neutral stance

Stand with your feet slightly more than a shoulder's width apart. This gives you a solid base, making it difficult for you to be knocked over. If your legs are too far apart or too close together, you'll be off-balance. One foot should be in front of the other, and your body should be turned slightly away from your opponent (so that you don't offer a huge target area). Bend your elbows and tuck them in to protect your ribcage. Your fists should remain near your jaw to protect your body and your head. (See figure 41, front view, and 42, side view.)

41

42

If you're right-handed, your left leg should be in front, and if you're left-handed your right leg should be in front. Thus, your most powerful kicks and punches will come from your strong side. In order to maintain balance, which is important in kickboxing, you should practice alternating with the left leg in front, then the right leg. This makes you develop necessary skills, so that during a sparring match, if you're forced to step back, you can still easily kick with whichever leg is forward—you don't have to switch your feet to be comfortable. It is important to remember this. You may naturally prefer to start your stance with the same foot forward each time, and this may be how you spar, but it is good practice to alternate legs so that you are ready for any situation you may find yourself in. This is especially important if you're thinking of your kickboxing training as a means of self-defense.

Although you kick with your front leg for speed, the most powerful kicks come from your back leg. The same with punching: you jab with your forward hand, but the powerful punches come from your back hand. Since the back leg kick is more powerful, it is considered the offensive kick; that is, you attack with kicks from your rear leg, attempting to score points and win the competition. The front leg kick, which is a speed kick, not a power kick, is considered a defensive kick. You use it to keep the opponent from coming toward you and landing kicks and punches.

When you perform kicks, you go through a series of movements. First, you chamber your leg, which means you position your leg to perform the kick. Then you perform the kick. Next, you re-chamber your leg (that is, return your leg to its starting position so that you can kick again if necessary). Finally, you set down your leg in the neutral stance position. Of course, this entire series of movements should be accomplished as quickly as possible, but it's important to understand how the technique is performed in order to do so correctly. If you fail to chamber or re-chamber your leg, you can create a sloppy kick that may throw you off balance, may not land in the targeted area, or may cause injury to your joints.

Abdominals

The abdominal region is not only the source of most of your power, it's also the center of stability (especially in women, who normally possess a lower center of gravity than men). Without strong abs, you rarely have a "fighting chance" in the ring or in a self-defense situation. You must train your abdominal muscles to keep them strong (see Chapter 13 for additional information.) The best way to obtain additional abdominal training (and to get that beautiful six-pack going) is to always tighten your abs during the execution (or exertion) phase of a technique. Try to pull your navel in toward your spine and pay attention to all the muscles in your abdominal region as you contract them. Training your "core" is as much a mental exercise as it is a physical one.

Eye contact

As you perform any technique, you must keep your eyes on your opponent. Some people make the mistake of looking directly at a specific target area on the opponent's body. An experienced fighter will read this signal, however, and know what you plan to do and will be able to defend against your attack. Also, if you're focusing on the target, such as the opponent's ribcage, you may not notice the punch coming at your head. Instead, look your opponent in the eye—objectify her! Although this may seem awkward at first, you will learn to use your peripheral vision to see what your opponent's arms and legs are doing. Maintain eye contact at all times when you're fighting in order to anticipate what your opponent is going to do, and to avoid telegraphing what you're going to do. Constant eye contact also provides the emotional advantage of perceived confidence, which can be quite intimidating to the opponent or attacker.

Striking accurately

When you perform a kick, make certain you strike with the correct part of your foot. Failure to do so can result in injury—to you! Also, strike to the correct target area. In kickboxing, this means the midsection or thighs. In a self-defense scenario, you could also strike to the knee or to the groin.

Chi

The development of chi (sometimes spelled "ki" or "qi") is as important in kickboxing as it is in traditional martial arts. Chi can be thought of as inner energy or focus. Think of it as residing in your abdomen (where your "core" stability comes from). When you use your chi, you can perform your strikes more powerfully and more accurately. Think of seeing yourself striking or kicking through the targeted area at the same time as you feel your chi or inner energy moving forward. To channel this energy correctly, you need to breathe properly as you perform your techniques. You should exhale as you strike (think of pushing the chi forward as you strike), and you should inhale as you re-chamber or return to your starting position. Focusing on your breathing prevents you from holding your breath (a problem many beginners have).

Center line

While the abdomen is the core of your strength, and your chi is the expression of that strength, your center line is your center of balance. Imagine a line going from the center of the top of your head through your body and exiting in the groin to meet the earth between your legs and feet. The center line is thrown off-balance if you step too far forward. If you lean too far back, again your center line is out of balance—and you're out of balance, too! If your spine is straight, your chin tucked and your pelvis slightly tilted forward, your center line will be correctly vertical. This concept is important to remember because if you lean too far forward (perhaps as you're punching) or too far back (perhaps as you avoid a kick) you can easily be pushed or pulled off balance or knocked over. Once you understand the basics of the neutral stance, abdominal or "core" strength, eye contact, the development of chi, correct breathing, and center line alignment, you're ready to start kicking.

Offensive front kick

The offensive front kick is a kick performed directly to a target in front of you, using your rear leg. Assume a fighter's stance. Chamber your rear leg by bringing it forward (toward your chest) and bending the knee tightly. A high, tight chamber generates more power and increases the range of target areas you can strike. Pull your toes back (remember this positioning from the ankle stretch) and point your foot. You will strike the target with the ball of your foot. Push your lower leg out, using your hips and your whole body to thrust forward. Strike to the target with the ball of your foot. Re-chamber your kick to the starting position. Return to the fighter's stance. Remember to maintain your guard and eye contact at all times as you execute each technique. (See figures 43–45).

43   *44*   *45*

46   47   48

Defensive front kick

The defensive front kick is performed directly to a target in front of you, using your forward (front) leg. It is performed in the same way as the offensive (rear leg) front kick. Assume a fighter's stance. Chamber your front leg by bringing it forward (toward your chest) and bending the knee tightly. Pull your toes back and point your foot. Push your lower leg out, using your hips and your whole body to thrust forward. Strike to the target with the ball of your foot. Re-chamber your kick to the starting position. Return to the fighter's stance. (See figures 46–48).

The defensive front kick is used to block the opponent's techniques. Sometimes you can just chamber your forward leg in the front kick position (figure 47) in order to block the opponent's strike. You can also use the kick the same way as the jab is used—to feel your opponent out and to test her defenses without committing to an offensive rear leg kick.

Offensive side kick

To perform the side kick, you turn your body to deliver a strike to an opponent in front of you. Although this makes the side kick a more complicated technique, this allows you to add more power to the kick. Assume a fighter's stance. Chamber your back leg as you did for the front kick, high and tight. However, as you chamber the kick, pivot on your supporting foot until your heel faces the target (that is, pivot 180 degrees). Lean your upper body back slightly so that your chambered leg is now parallel to the floor. The foot of your kicking leg should be pulled back so that your heel is closest to the target. This is the striking surface

49   50   51

52   53   54

for the side kick. Your foot should be straight or with toes turned slightly down. If your toes are turned up, you'll end up striking with your toes or the sole of your foot rather than the heel of your foot, and you could injure yourself. Snap your leg toward the target, striking with your heel. Re-chamber your kick, then set your foot down in the fighter's stance. (See figures 49–51.)

Defensive side kick

The defensive side kick can be used to feel your opponent out. It can also be used to block a strike or to prevent your opponent from moving in on you. Chamber your forward leg, bending your knee tightly. Pivot on your supporting foot as you chamber (at the moment of impact, you should have pivoted 180 degrees), strike to the target with your heel. (See figure 49–51.)

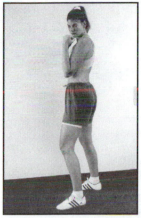

55   56   57

Offensive roundhouse kick

This kick is sometimes called a round kick. You can use it to strike to all target areas. Not only is the offensive round kick powerful, but with practice, it's very fast—so fast your opponent may not see it coming. In this kick, your instep or the front part of your shin is the striking surface.

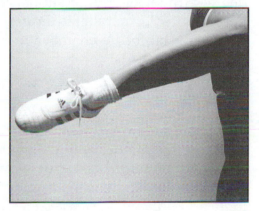

58

Assume the fighter's stance. Chamber your rear leg in a high and tight chamber. Pivot on the ball of your supporting foot (as you do for the side kick) 180 degrees, so that the heel of your supporting foot faces the target. Your kicking leg should be parallel to the ground. Sweep the lower part of your leg toward the target. Thus, your leg moves in a semicircular motion from chamber to target area. Re-chamber your leg and return to the fighter's stance. (See figures 55–58).

Defensive roundhouse kick

Like the offensive roundhouse kick, the defensive roundhouse kick can be used to strike to all target areas, but it is most effective when used defensively, to jab at your opponent, to open up her defenses, and to vary your kicking arsenal. It is performed the same as the offensive roundhouse kick, only you use your forward leg to kick. Chamber your forward leg in a high and tight chamber. Pivot on your supporting foot 180

| 59 | 60 | 61 |

degrees (the heel of your supporting foot should face the target). Keep your kicking leg parallel to the ground. Sweep the lower part of your leg toward the target. Re-chamber your leg and return to the fighter's stance. (See figures 59–61).

Turn back kick

Sometimes called the back kick or the reverse side kick, the turn back kick is not used very often in sparring and it should never be used as an attacking technique, only to counter an opponent's technique. It is an extremely powerful kick, but because you turn away from your opponent, thus leaving you vulnerable to an attack, it should be used sparingly and only when you see the perfect opening. Like the sidekick, this technique uses the heel of your foot to strike.

Assume a fighter's stance. Pivot on both feet so that your heels face your target. Look over your shoulder to keep an eye on your target. You are now coiled and ready to unleash the kick. Bring the leg farthest from the target up in a high and tight chamber. Strike to the target with the heel of your foot. Re-chamber your leg and assume the fighter's stance. You can set your kicking foot down so that it becomes the forward leg, or you can continue the revolution and set your kicking leg down so that it becomes the rear leg. If you make it the forward leg, you will be in a slightly different fighter's stance. (For instance, if you started the kick with your left leg forward in the fighter's stance, you will now have your right leg forward). By doing this, you protect yourself from a possible counter-attack. However, it can be confusing to you as a fighter to suddenly have a different leg forward. If you make the kicking leg the rear leg, you will be in the same fighter's stance as when you started, but by continuing the revolution this additional half-turn, you expose

62 63 64 65

yourself to a counter-attack. Thus, many fighters choose to make the kicking leg their forward leg, assuming that switching things around occasionally is good practice. (See figures 62–65).

FOR WOMEN ONLY: Women have very strong hips and legs, especially in comparison to their upper body strength. Therefore, they have an advantage in kickboxing: they can perform powerful kicking techniques right away. All it requires is practice.

FOR WOMEN ONLY: Women tend to be more flexible than men, which means you'll be able to kick to a greater range of target areas. This is important especially in self-defense scenarios where an attacker may be quite a bit taller and heavier than you are. In the kickboxing ring, you may be able to kick to an opponent's head, which is not very common, incorporates the element of surprise and is a good way to gain an advantage in competition.

DEBZ SAYS: To understand how to "channel" your chi, think of your chi as water flowing under pressure through a small hose from the center of your body out through the part of your body that is striking the target. The "water" doesn't dribble, and the "hose" doesn't have a kink in it—instead, your chi comes out in a rush to help generate power and accuracy.

6
KNEE STRIKES

Knee strikes are an effective weapon for women since they generate a great deal of power, no matter how big or small you are. You can target legs, chest or head with knee strikes. There are two types of knee strikes: the straight knee strike and the side knee strike. Both are performed using the rear leg for power and balance. Both are easier to perform if you grab your opponent's head or neck, although you don't have to. Not only does grabbing your opponent help you maintain your balance, but you can pull your attacker into the strike, thus increasing its effectiveness.

Straight knee strike

Assume a fighter's stance. Lock both hands around your opponent's neck. Lift your back leg and drive your knee straight into the target area. The kneecap is your striking surface. (See figures 66–68).

Side knee strike

Assume a fighter's stance. Place both hands on your opponent's neck. Lift your back leg so that your thigh is parallel to the floor. Bend your

66

67

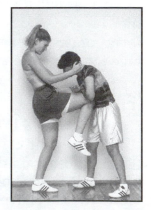

68

69

70

knee to a 90 degree angle. Pull your opponent toward you. At the same time, sweep your knee toward your target, keeping it in the same 90 degree position. The inside of your lower thigh is the actual striking surface. (See figures 69–70).

FOR WOMEN ONLY: For self-defense, use a straight knee strike to the groin to disable an attacker. This is a fast and efficient method for getting loose from someone who grabs you.

DEBZ SAYS: Knee strikes soften up your opponent in no time. The side knee strike is extremely powerful, even when small women use it. Move quickly, though, or your opponent will be able to strike to your unprotected chest. To help prevent this, keep your elbows tucked in toward your ribs even as you grab your opponent's head to pull it toward you.

7
PUNCHES

Punches are the unsung heroes of the kickboxer's arsenal. With them, you're able to fight in close range. You can target punches more accurately than kicks, and punches are faster to perform than kicks. For these reasons, it makes sense to perfect your punches even though the kicks might be more fun.

Most women feel their upper body strength is not as good as it could be. This doesn't mean you can't punch effectively. It just means you have some additional work to do. As you train in kickboxing, you may need to do some weight lifting to build your upper body, or you may simply do conditioning exercises (such as push-ups) to increase strength (see Chapter 13 for more information). You can also generate power by performing punches correctly and by using the entire weight of your body behind each punch.

To make a fist, roll your fingers into a tight ball. The outer surface of your fist should be flat. Secure the fist by bending your thumb across your fingers. The first two knuckles (nearest the thumb) are the striking surface. Don't try to strike with the whole fist, since that will cause you to tilt your wrist and could cause injury. And don't strike with the last two knuckles, since they are the smallest and will swell, even break, if you strike with them repeatedly.

Boxers use their dominant hand to deliver the power punches such as crosses and uppercuts. Thus, a right-handed boxer would use her right hand to deliver the power punches. She would stand with her left leg slightly forward. But kickboxers should practice using both sides evenly, so remember to alternate as you train; sometimes your left foot should be forward and you should deliver your power punches with your right hand, and sometimes your right foot should be forward and you should deliver your power punches from your left hand. This will also ensure that any muscles you build will be evenly balanced.

As you practice punching, your first goal is to perform the technique correctly and accurately. These means the mechanics of punching should be performed as perfectly as possible. You should shift your weight and execute the punch as described. You should strike the target you're aiming for. If this means punching at a slightly slower rate than seems effective, that's fine. As you build confidence, you can work at a higher rate of speed.

Practice punching to different target areas, such as the chin, the nose, the jaw, the chest and the abdomen. If you're working on a heavy bag, strike three or four times to the middle section, then three or four times to the head, then back to the middle section. By mixing it up, you'll be in a position to dominate your opponent. Also, the more times you make contact with the opponent, the better the chances of neurologically "short-circuiting" her, giving you an advantage.

Jab

The jab is a fast punch used to set up power punches. Although you won't land a knockout punch with a jab, it can be a powerful weapon in itself, wearing out the opponent. Mainly, though, it is used to draw the opponent's guard away so that you can land a power punch to an unguarded target.

Assume a fighter's stance. Make your hands into fists, guarding your jaw, chin tucked, arms close to the body. This is the chamber position.

71

72

73   74   75

With your forward hand, strike to the target, spiraling the fist from the starting position (fingers facing your head) toward the opponent (palm facing down), keeping your arm about shoulder level. At the same time, shift some of your weight to your forward leg. This adds power to your punch. Keep your elbow slightly bent in order to absorb the shock of the blow (otherwise you can jam or hyperextend the joint. This is painful). Re-chamber your arm quickly and return to your starting position. (See figures 71–72).

Cross

This is sometimes called the straight punch. Use this punch in combination with the jab—jab first, then strike with the cross. The cross usually targets the head, although it can be used to strike to the body as well.

Assume a fighter's stance. Make your hands into fists, guarding your jaw, using the same proper body alignment as described for the jab. This is the chamber position. With your rear hand, strike toward the target. Keep your arm about shoulder level as you punch. If you're aiming for the body, drop your body instead of dropping your arm to hit the target area—that is, bend your knees as you punch. At the same time you throw the punch, shift your weight to your forward leg, pivoting on your feet. Your rear hip should rotate with the punch, providing more power and stability. Again, keep your elbow slightly bent to absorb the shock of the blow. Re-chamber your arm quickly and return to the starting position. (See figures 73–75).

76   77   78

Hook

The hook can be performed with either the forward or the rear hand. From the rear it is more powerful, but using the forward hand, it can be performed in a quick combination with the cross.

Assume a fighter's stance. Make your hands into fists, guarding your jaw. Bend the elbow of your punching arm so that it creates a 90 degree angle. Your arm should be at shoulder level, parallel to the floor. Pivot your upper body into the punch, rotating from the hip. The fist, elbow, shoulder, hip and feet should all pivot as one connected, flowing movement. Do NOT flail the arm outward! Don't move your arm at all; your body does all the work. Return to the starting position. To guard best from this position, point the elbow of your guarding hand upward so the fist is near your ear and the rest of your arm is protecting the side of your face and head.

The hook can target the head as well as the body. To strike to the body, don't drop your arm, but again, bend your knees more and lower your body into the punch. (See figures 76–78).

Uppercut

The uppercut strikes upward instead of directly to the target. You can use the forward or the rear hand to perform the technique. It is most powerful when it is performed with the rear hand, but the forward hand can be used to make an effective combination of cross, then uppercut.

Assume a fighter's stance. Keep your hands up, guarding your jaw. Bend at the knees. Drop your punching arm slightly past shoulder level.

Pivot, shifting your weight to your forward leg. Strike directly upward with the punch. Re-chamber and return to the starting position. The uppercut can strike to the body or the underside of the chin. Again, lower your body when you want to punch to the body, and use a more upright position if you want to punch to the head. (See figure 79–80).

The uppercut is one of the most difficult punches to develop correctly. To understand the mechanics of this punch, think of how a piston in an internal combustion engine works, rotating a little on the downward stroke, then exploding straight upward on the finishing stroke.

79   80

Overhand punch

This punch is designed to get past the guard of your opponent when no other punch will. Its drawback is that it leaves your body open for the opponent to strike. That means you should use it only when your other punches keep getting deflected. The punch is thrown with your rear hand.

Assume a fighter's stance. Launch the punch with your rear fist at an upward angle (rather than straight from the shoulder). Pivot as you punch, shifting your weight to your forward foot. As you strike, you will shift your arm so that your fist comes down on the target. This means the punch travels in an arc; first, slightly upward, then down to the target. Re-chamber your hands and return to the starting position. (See figures 81–83).

81   82   83

Spinning backfist

Like the turn back kick, this technique requires that you turn your back on your opponent, so that you are momentarily "blind." Although this is a powerful technique, that moment of blindness can be a major drawback, so you must use the spinning backfist only when conditions are right. You have to be fast and accurate; if not, your opponent will take advantage.

Assume a fighter's stance. Your rear fist will perform the actual strike, and you will use the back of your fist as the striking surface. Rotate to the back. Turn your head over your shoulder as you rotate so that you can see your target. As you turn, extend your striking arm almost parallel to the floor. Keep your elbow slightly bent to avoid injury. As you continue to rotate around, strike to the target with the back of your fist. Like the turn back kick, you can either continue rotating until you are back at your starting position, or you can stop, with your opposite foot (and arm) forward. The first option leaves you vulnerable to a counter-attack (your body may be exposed as you continue turning), so the second option, assuming a fighter's stance with the opposite leg forward, is usually chosen. (See figures 84–86).

Punching Drill

In order to stay protected, kickboxers must learn to perform punches while remaining in a guarded position. This is a difficult concept to understand at first. To practice, wad up several large pieces of newspaper. Place one wad under your chin and hold it there. Place one wad under

84

85

86

87

88

each of your armpits. Hold each wad of newspaper in position. Then, perform each of the punches as described without dropping any of the newspaper. This is extremely difficult to do at first, but once you can perform all of the punches without dropping the newspaper, you're getting the hang of keeping your chin tucked and your elbows in, which helps you maintain a guarded position. (See figures 87–88).

FOR WOMEN ONLY: Long fingernails make it difficult to make a fist. Without a fist, you can't punch. Getting rid of the fingernails will prevent accidental injury (to yourself when your nails dig into your palms and to your partner when your nails accidentally claw her face).

FOR WOMEN ONLY: Women's knuckles are smaller than men's and usually can't take as much abuse. Since you don't want swollen or broken knuckles, take extra care to punch with the first two knuckles of your fist (the biggest knuckles, nearest your thumb). Also, be sure to wrap your hands and to spend some time punching the heavy bag to help condition your hands before you start pounding on opponents.

FOR WOMEN ONLY: Women can usually perform techniques quickly. This is a great asset for punching, even though it may seem that a powerful upper body is more important. It's not. Much of the snap and power of a punch comes from your hand speed. Your hand speed is the combination of how long it takes you to launch the punch, land the punch, and return your hand to the starting position. Challenge yourself to return your hand to the starting position faster than you struck with it. This prevents lazy habits like dropping your hands after you punch, and it also ensures that your punches sting the opponent rather than just push at her.

DEBZ SAYS: Remember, visualization is an important key to the success of the kickboxer. Really think about and picture in your mind's eye each punch traveling THROUGH the targeted area. You'll be amazed at how much more powerful and precise your punches become!

8
RULES TO REMEMBER

In kickboxing competition, certain techniques, such as elbow strikes, are illegal—that is, you could lose the match just for using the technique. Some target areas, such as the groin, are also illegal. Even though you can't use elbow strikes or strike to the groin in competition, it makes sense to practice them because they can help you in a self-defense situation. However, you have to remember that you can get disqualified (and hurt yourself or your opponent) if you use them in competition.

In general, kicks, punches and knees strikes can be used to the thighs, the head (including the jaw, the nose, and the sides of the head) and the midsection, including the ribcage, the chest and the abdomen. Some techniques are more effective against certain target areas. For example, some kicks, like the front kick, lose a lot of power if you try to kick high with them. You can also lose your balance. Therefore, it's usually better to use a front kick to kick to the middle section or to the thighs. The sidekick, turn back kick and knee strikes are similar; it is best to use them to strike to the middle section. The roundhouse kick can be used to strike to the head, if you're flexible enough (and many women are or can easily become this flexible). As far as the punches go, all of them are effective if you punch to the head. The cross, hook and uppercut can also target the body to soften up the opponent.

Elbow strikes

Although illegal in all but Muay Thai competition, elbow strikes can be useful in self-defense situations, so it pays to practice them. There are two striking areas on the elbow: the front of the elbow and the point of the elbow. Every elbow strike uses one or the other of these striking surfaces. You can perform an elbow strike using the forward arm or the rear arm. The rear arm elbow strike generates more power but the forward arm elbow strike is faster.

89   90

Forward elbow strike

This strike uses the front of the elbow as the striking surface. Bend the arm tightly. Keep your arm horizontal to the floor. Pivoting at the waist, using the full power of the rotation of your hips, reach back behind you with the elbow, then sweep your elbow forward and through the target. Return to the starting position. (See figures 89–90). This technique usually targets the head.

Reverse elbow strike

This technique uses the point of your elbow as the striking surface. The target is directly behind you. Bend your arm so that it is at a 90 degree angle with your forearm horizontal to the floor. Make your hand a fist. Reach forward slightly with your arm, then shove backward with your elbow, driving the point of your elbow into the target.

You can increase the power of this technique by sliding backward as you execute the elbow strike, which puts the entire weight of your body behind it. This technique is used to the body, especially the abdomen. (See figures 91–92).

Upward elbow strike

This technique uses the front of the elbow as the striking surface. Bend your arm tightly so that the point of your elbow faces toward the floor. Make your hand into a fist. Sweep the elbow upward. Strike with the front (now the top) part of the elbow.

You can increase the power of this technique by sliding or stepping forward as you execute it. This puts the entire weight of your body

91   92

behind the technique. As with the uppercut, it is valuable to imitate the action of a piston to gain the most from this strike. Then return to the starting position. This technique is most effective when it strikes the underside of the target, such as the jaw. (See figures 93–94).

93   94

Side elbow strike

This technique uses the point of the elbow as the striking surface. The target is to the side. Bend your arm so that it creates a 90 degree angle. Make your hand a fist. Bring your arm slightly across your body. Drive your elbow to the side, into the target. Then return to the starting position.

95 96

To increase the power of this technique, you can step or slide to the side as you perform it. This puts the weight of your body into the technique. This technique targets the ribcage or abdomen. (See figures 95–96).

FOR WOMEN ONLY: Practice doing elbow strikes full power by having an opponent hold a kicking target while you strike. Ask your partner to tell you when he or she thinks you're striking hard enough to do damage to an attacker.

FOR WOMEN ONLY: Practice performing front kicks to the groin to stop an attacker. Instead of pushing your foot forward when you kick to the groin, sweep your foot upward so that the instep of your foot hits the target (rather than using your toes). This makes the front kick more effective against an attacker.

DEBZ SAYS: When you practice "illegal" techniques with a partner, be sure your partner knows what you're doing! Communicate, communicate, communicate! This is the best way to prevent an accident from happening.

9
BLOCKING AND EVADING

Once you've learned to use the striking techniques in kickboxing, you have to learn how to avoid them when you're fighting. Such defensive moves are key to your survival and success in the ring. Blocking and evading are defensive techniques used to keep your opponent from doing too much damage. Evading techniques are used to avoid a strike entirely, such as by moving out of the way. Blocking techniques are used to intercept a strike so that it does not land on a more vulnerable area. Blocking allows you to get hit without receiving too much damage.

In order to block effectively, you need to maintain a good fighter's stance at all times. This means keeping your weight balanced evenly between both legs, and keeping your arms up, your elbows tucked into your ribcage, your fists guarding your face and your chin tucked. Whenever you strike with a kick or punch, you return your hand or foot to the starting position as soon as possible in order to keep your guard up and defend against a counter-attack.

From this position, if a strike comes toward your face, you can easily move your hand slightly to protect your face. If the blow comes toward your body you can move your arm or drop your elbow to protect yourself. You can use any part of your body to block, although blocking with your head is probably counterproductive. A kick that lands on your forearm hurts much less than one that lands on your head.

To perform blocks most effectively, you have to understand that your opponent will strike you with either a sweeping, circular technique or a direct technique. A circular technique such as the roundhouse kick moves from one side to another in an arc. Direct techniques, such as the front kick, move directly to the target. To determine how to block an attack, you have to know whether it's a circular attack or a direct attack. With some experience, you will be able to tell this in a split second.

Catching

You can block a technique by catching it. You usually perform this block with your rear hand, while pivoting away from the opponent (this is so if you miss, you won't get hit). The catch can be used against any type of attack, but it is limited. Once you've caught someone's punch, you can't effectively counterattack until you let go of their hand, and by then the momentum and movement has been lost. (See figure 97.) To prevent this, follow up by using the hooking technique to change the direction of the oncoming punch. (See below).

97

Hooking

After stopping the punch with a catch, move your palm downward and outward in a circular motion. This moves the opponent's punch off angle and opens up her centerline, leaving her vulnerable to your counterattack. (See figures 98–99).

98

99

Cupping

Cupping is another useful defensive technique against an oncoming punch, but it is usually reserved for women who are taller and faster

100 *101*

than their opponents. As the punch comes toward you, push against it from above, palm down, changing the momentum so that it is directed downward. You can also cup a punch from below (palm up) if you're taller and have a lot of speed. Remember, cupping only changes the direction of the punch so that it goes up or down. When you use this technique, you can open up your centerline, leaving yourself vulnerable to a counter-attack, so use it wisely! (See figures 100–101).

Parrying

To parry a strike, you deflect it away from you instead of catching it. Essentially, you swat the technique away with your arm, turning your body into it as you move. This works best for direct attacks. You may also use a small, tight, circular motion with your hand to "brush" away the oncoming technique. Don't overcommit to the parry, however, or your opponent will take advantage. Let the strike come to you; don't go chasing it. (This requires trusting your reflexes, which comes with experience.) Move the opponent's arm or foot out of the way just enough so that the technique does not land on your body. Parrying kicks is a little more hazardous than parrying punches: if you drop your arm in order to move the opponent's leg out of the way, you leave your body open to a counter attack from your opponent. Working on speed will help you with this. You usually parry with the arm closest to your opponent's attack. That is, if your opponent strikes with her left arm or leg, you will parry with your right arm. (See figures 102–103).

102   103

Parry guard

Because parrying can leave you vulnerable to a counter-attack, work on a special guard for use when you parry. Move your rear hand toward your opposite shoulder as you step to the side out of the way of the punch. The thumb of your rear hand, your opposite shoulder and your tucked chin work together to guard against counter-attack. (See figure 104.)

The blocking techniques described above require simple movements of your arms to protect the vulnerable parts of your anatomy. But these techniques won't be enough to block every attack. You will also need to learn some additional techniques, especially to defend against kicks.

104   105

106

Shin block

When someone kicks toward you, you can lift your forward leg, bending the knee at a 90 degree angle, and stop the kick from traveling in by blocking it with your shin. This works for both circular kicks and direct kicks. (See figure 105.)

Knee-elbow block

Similar to the shin block, use this technique if you're not certain where the attacker plans to strike. Lift your forward leg, bending the knee at a 90 degree angle. At the same time, bend the elbow of your forward arm to a 90 degree angle. Touch your elbow to your knee, keeping your hand close to your head and jaw. This protects almost all potential target areas. However, it is difficult to counter-attack from this position, so the knee-elbow block should only be used as a last resort. (See figure 106.)

Double arm block

This is a technique boxers use to protect their heads. Simply raise both arms, lower your head and let the opponent's punches hit your arms. This technique leaves your body open, so you should only use it for a few moments to regroup, wait for an opening and counter-attack. (See figure 107.)

107

108

Reinforced double arm block

This is a variation of the double arm block technique. Use this technique if your opponent is kicking to your head (most likely with a roundhouse kick). Since this is a more powerful technique than a punch, a one-arm block may not be sufficient to stop the force of the kick. Instead, cross both arms to protect your head from the kick, using one hand to reinforce the other. Like the double arm block, this leaves your body open, so you should use it only occasionally, when you need a quick block before you counter-attack. (See figure 108.)

109

Clinch

This is a technique that boxers use when they get too tired in the ring to spar effectively. In essence, you grab your opponent, securing her arms against your body and move in close. This prevents your opponent from kicking you. However, she may still be able to punch at you. You can deliver knee strikes using this technique. It is really only a desperate defensive maneuver, but one worth knowing about. (See figure 109.)

Thai thigh block

Use this technique to change the direction of a kick. Lift your leg, bending your knee tightly. Sweep your leg inward or outward, pushing the opponent's foot away as you move. (See figure 110.)

110

111

112

Forearm-elbow block

Use your forearm and elbow to sweep either a punch or a kick out of the way, pivoting your body as you sweep. You can sweep your forearm and elbow in a side-to-side movement or in a downward movement. (See figure 111.)

Sometimes a block is all you can do to protect yourself from a strike. But there are better ways to protect yourself from getting hit. One of the best ways is to use evasive techniques. By evading a punch, you never make physical contact with your opponent (and, of course, she never makes physical contact with you!). Not getting hit at all is better than blocking a kick or punch.

Boxers use an evasive technique called the "bob-and-weave" to make their opponents miss them. To evade your opponent's punches and kicks, you have to focus on your opponent and anticipate where she is going to strike. This comes with experience.

Ducking

This technique is straightforward. You see a technique come toward you and you duck to avoid it. Ducking works best against sweeping techniques, such as hooks and roundhouse kicks. Someone performing a direct technique, such as a cross, may still be able to make contact if you duck. In addition, if you don't protect yourself as you duck, your opponent may be able to perform a knee strike or other technique to your head.

Instead of leaning forward or away to duck, bend your knees and squat. Keep your hands up guarding your face to protect it from a knee strike or similar attack. Work to move into and out of the squat position quickly. (See figure 112.)

After you've ducked your opponent's technique, you should counter with a strike of your own. Successful counter-attacks after ducking include the uppercut and the upward elbow strike.

Slipping

When you slip a punch, you merely turn your body to avoid the technique. This requires less energy on your part than ducking does and gives the opponent a smaller target. It also allows you to set up a counter-

113

114

attack. If you turn your body aside to slip a punch, you can counter-attack with a powerful strike as you move your body back to your starting position.

To slip, pivot on your feet away from the punch, turning your shoulder at the same time so that you present the side of your body to your opponent. (See figures 113–114). This technique can be used no matter what side your attacker is punching toward.

Duck and slip

You can pair the techniques of ducking and slipping to avoid your attacker's strikes. As your attacker punches, duck slightly and pivot away from the punch. Unlike simply ducking, this technique allows you to counter-attack quickly and leaves you less vulnerable to follow-up attacks by your opponent. (See figure 115.)

115

Footwork is also used to evade your opponent's attacks. Footwork is simply how you move and place your feet as you fight. Good footwork can move you out of the way of an attack and move you back in to counter-attack. The basic idea is to be light on your feet as you're moving around the ring, waiting for your opponent to attack, looking for an opening. Only when you actually defend against an attack or attack your opponent will you "plant" yourself so that you don't lose balance or become easy to push over. Remember your center line: stay vertical in order to stay balanced.

To stay light on your feet, practice moving around on the balls of your feet. Not only is this good practice for your footwork, it is good practice for your kicks. Since you often pivot on the ball of your foot to perform a kick (and in the case of the front kick, you actually use the ball of your foot as the striking surface), this is an extremely important skill to learn. Too often, fighters stand flatfooted and kick flatfooted. They pivot on the whole of their foot. If you pivot on your whole foot, you slow your kick down. Some actually pivot on their heels or toes. If you pivot on your heels or toes, you cannot perform kicks appropriately and you risk off balancing yourself, making it easier for your opponent to take advantage.

It can be difficult to get used to moving around on the balls of your feet, so practice every chance you get—as you walk around the house, as you work, as you shop, you can practice walking on the balls of your feet. This practice will also strengthen the muscles in your feet so that you don't get tired in the ring when you must move around on the balls of your feet or you won't move fast enough.

Footwork refers to the position and movement of your feet. By following certain footwork patterns, you can move into and out of fighting range against an opponent. Footwork also helps you avoid your opponent's techniques. Practice each pattern repeatedly, both separately and as a part of your sparring practice. This will help you understand the purpose of each pattern. If you have a partner, she can punch or kick at you while you practice footwork techniques.

Center line drill

To stay light on your feet while remaining balanced, you have to keep your center line vertical. To practice this, use the following Tai Chi standing meditation exercise. Stand in a relaxed position, with your center line straight and arms slightly bent in front (as if you were hugging a tree). Close your eyes. Concentrate on deeply inhaling for at least 6–8 counts, then hold your breathe for 4 counts, then exhale for 6–8 counts. While inhaling, visualize the air going all the way into your feet. Then imagine your feet sprouting roots into the earth. As you hold your breath and then exhale it, visualize these roots growing thicker and stronger, helping you become more stable. The purpose of the exercise is to become completely relaxed while remaining firm and immovable. The more adept you become at this, the more your mind and body "remember" the feeling of immovability and it will be much easier to maintain balance while remaining light on your feet.

Forward stepping

Use forward stepping (also called straight stepping or shuffling) when you need to move into kicking or punching range. Slide your front foot forward, then slide your back foot forward. Practice making small, quick

116

117

118

119

120

121

sliding movements toward your target. Be prepared to stop your forward motion in a split-second, in case your opponent responds to your movement. (See figures 116–118.) To cover your movement, you can perform a kick with your forward leg, then set your foot down closer to your opponent (rather than re-chambering it and returning it to the starting position). Then slide your back foot forward. (See figures 119–120.)

Backward stepping

This technique merely reverses the sequence of steps in forward stepping. Use backward stepping to get out of range of your opponent's attacks and to move into punching or kicking range if you're too close to your opponent to attack effectively. Slide your back foot backward, then your front foot. Practice this technique using quick sliding movements. Again, you can use a kick to cover your movement. In this case, use your front leg to kick, then set your kicking foot down next to your back foot and slide your back foot back. (See figures 122–124.).

122

123

124

Combine techniques

Combine forward stepping and backward stepping to move into and out of fighting range. Be sure you *don't* get into a rhythm (two forward steps, two backward steps, two forward steps...) because this is easy for an opponent to respond to. Instead, vary the way you combine the two techniques so that your opponent cannot predict whether you're coming or going.

Switch stepping

Use this technique to change which leg is the forward leg. Being able to do this facilitates kicking. Keeping light on your feet, quickly shuffle your feet so that your forward foot become your rear foot and your rear foot becomes your forward foot. As you becomes more comfortable with this technique, you can add a kick as you perform the switch. (See figures 125–126).

125

126

Side stepping

Use this pattern to move out of the way of a direct attack. Instead of stepping backward, use a quick step to the side. This can be used in combination with ducking or slipping. Unlike backward stepping, side stepping keeps you in range so that you can immediately counter your opponent's attack. To step left, simply slide your forward foot to the left and follow with your back foot. Again, use a sliding motion that can easily be stopped and redirected in case you need to respond to a movement on your opponent's part.

You must move in the direction *opposite* the strike in order to evade it. Therefore, if a kick is coming toward the left side of your body, you must move to the right. Otherwise, you will step into the kick and suffer for it. Practice sidestepping a variety of techniques so that you can get a sense of the intended target area of a strike before you try to avoid it. Once you can avoid a strike by sidestepping it, add a countering technique of your own. For example, if your opponent punches toward your right shoulder and you step to the left, you can deliver a side kick to her now-exposed ribs. Practice the sidestepping and the countering moves repeatedly, until you feel comfortable with them. Then incorporate them into your sparring practice. (See figures 127–130).

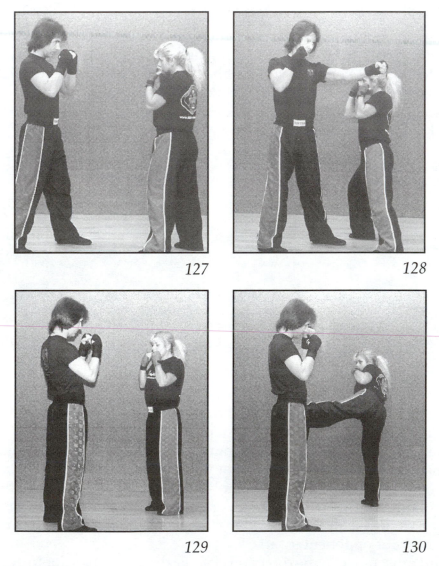

127

128

129

130

Pivot stepping

Use the pivot step to move toward or away from your opponent. Unlike forward and backward stepping, you do not have to make a complete commitment to the direction you plan to travel. Because of this, pivot stepping gives you more flexibility, but it is more difficult to learn.

To pivot step toward your opponent and move into fighting range, push off with your rear foot and pivot toward your opponent on the ball of your front foot (your supporting foot). Your rear foot then becomes your forward foot. If you need to move out of the way of an attack, you can then pivot on your "new" forward foot, sliding your back foot behind you, allowing an attack to slide by. Be certain that you do not pivot step *into* an opponent's attack. This requires practice. (See figures 131–132).

To pivot step away from your opponent and move out of fighting range, push off with your forward foot and pivot in a semi-circle on your back foot. Your back foot then becomes your front foot. You are then farther from your opponent, and his attack can slide right by you. Pivot stepping away from an opponent works best when the opponent is overwhelming you, and you need to move out of the way without

131

132

133

134

appearing to be retreating. This gives you a moment to regroup and launch your own attack. You can pivot step several times in a row, both moving forward and moving backward. This gives you greater control over your fighting range.

Use pivot stepping in sparring since turning your back on an opponent to avoid a blow (while sometimes tempting) is dangerous. (See figures 133–134).

Advancing and retreating triangle stepping

Instead of moving in, out, or to the side, you can move at an angle (either forward or backward). This step helps you avoid an opponent's strike while remaining in range to strike yourself.

As the opponent kicks or punches, avoid the strike by sliding your forward foot at a 45 degree angle to your opponent (moving to the side opposite of the strike). Then slide your back foot into position and strike to your opponent's unguarded side. (See figures 135–136).

135

136

137

You can move backward, away from the opponent (again at a 45 degree angle), to avoid a strike. Use this technique to move out of close range and into kicking range. In this case, move your back foot first, following with your forward foot. (See figure 137). As you move you back foot, you can put your weight on that foot and kick with your forward foot to your opponent's unguarded side.

Fighting range

Fighting range is an important concept to learn. Not only does it help you understand what techniques to use and when, it also helps you anticipate what techniques your opponent will use and when. If the distance between you and your opponent in the ring is so great that you can't kick or punch, you're outside of fighting range.

If you're closer, just a few feet away, you're in kicking range. A kick will strike your opponent, but a hand technique will be too far away for effectiveness. When you're about 18 to 24 inches away from your opponent, you're in punching range. If you're slightly closer, you're in knee and elbow range. If you're only a few inches apart, you're again out of fighting range, since none of the techniques you could try would be effective. (See figures 138–143 on the following page).

Good fighters learn how to move into and out of the various fighting ranges in order to take advantage of the techniques they do well. When you practice sparring, pay particular attention to fighting ranges. You will learn that once you kick, you are or can easily be in punching range, so it makes sense to put together combinations of techniques that start with a kick, continue with a punch and end with a knee or elbow strike.

You can use footwork techniques to move into and out of different fighting ranges. Use the patterns previously described (forward stepping, backward stepping, side stepping) to move into and out of different ranges in order to use your techniques most effectively.

These blocking and evading techniques should be practiced with a partner. Have a partner throw different punches and kicks to your head and body, starting slowly at first and then building up speed. As your partner strikes, try ducking, slipping and blocking the techniques. Or, have a partner use a focus mitt and swipe at your head and body with it as you try to block or evade it. (See figures 144–145.)

Shadow boxing

You can also do shadow boxing drills by practicing the techniques by yourself (use a mirror to make sure your body position is correct). This will help you get a feel for what your body should be doing. Simply

138

139

140

141

142

143

imagine that someone is attacking you with various kicks and punches and practice ducking, slipping, blocking and using footwork to avoid these phantom strikes. Shadow sparring is also an excellent way to practice the techniques of kickboxing and to practice putting them together

144   145

in combinations (which will be discussed in the next three chapters). It's good practice to shadow box for two or three minute rounds, just as you would in competition. This helps condition your body and trains you not to let up even if you're getting tired.

You can also use slow motion shadow sparring to warm up before a workout. Once you break a light sweat, you can start stretching and then move into the workout itself. One great benefit of shadow sparring is that you can do it anywhere. Although it helps to have a mirror so that you can see what you're doing, you can shadow spar in the kitchen while you're waiting for the microwave to finish thawing two pounds of chicken breasts or in a hotel room when you're traveling for business, or in your office when you've just had a stressful meeting with your boss.

FOR WOMEN ONLY: Since women tend to injure their knees more frequently than men do, take the extra time to strengthen the muscles around your knee. You'll need this extra protection for performing the ducking, slipping and footwork techniques described in this chapter, since many of them rely on extensive bending and twisting of your knees. The footwork drills used in conjunction with keeping the center line vertical will improve your quadriceps strength, which is very important in preventing knee stress and injury.

FOR WOMEN ONLY: Women tend to be more agile and flexible than men. Put these qualities to good use by learning the techniques of evasion and footwork. Not getting hit at all is much better than executing perfect blocks!

DEBZ SAYS: Dancing is a perfect background for kickboxing. You have to stay light on your feet, move around, and pay attention to your partner. This makes hitting the dance clubs on Fridays excusable as part of your training regimen. Just remember to cool it on the alcohol consumption, which greatly decreases your capability and reduces training progress!

10
KICK COMBINATIONS

Most beginning fighters spar in a predictable way: they'll perform one kick, then wait for their opponent/partner to kick. Then they'll punch one time and wait for their opponent to punch. This is no way to win a fight. Instead, you need to concentrate on performing more than one technique in a row. In this way, you can overwhelm your opponent just by sheer persistence. Keep going after your opponent and eventually her guard will drop, and you can score that knockout blow.

Even if you're not the aggressive, attacking fighter described above, you can use kick combinations to defeat your opponent by forcing her to counter-attack, at which time, you can counter-attack. You can use kick combinations to get a feel for your opponent's defenses without leaving yourself open to a serious counter-attack. But to perform kicks in combination you have to have a plan and a little experience. You have to know when you strike with your first kick what your next kick will (or might) be. You must also use compatible kicks in combination. For example, performing a defensive front kick followed by a turn back kick doesn't work very well. The kicks don't flow naturally together. With experience, you'll be able to judge what kicks work best in what combinations. This varies some from fighter to fighter, and as you gain more experience, you gain more options.

When you do kicking combinations, you usually use your front leg for the first kick. This is sort of like a jab. You can feel your opponent out first. If she takes the bait, you follow up with the second kick (as you had planned) which will be a powerful, payoff kick. If she doesn't take the bait or counter-attacks, you can re-think your strategy, but you haven't over-committed yourself or left your body unguarded.

The combinations described below make excellent kicking combinations. You may devise others. Although the combinations described only consist of two kicks, you should also have a plan for what happens after the second kick: another kick? A punch? Always concentrate on doing more than one or two techniques in a row.

Front kick-roundhouse kick combination

From the fighter's stance, perform a defensive front kick (with your forward leg). Return your leg to its starting position and immediately launch a roundhouse kick with your rear leg. The front kick may cause your opponent to drop her hands, in which case you should perform the roundhouse kick to her now unguarded head. (See figures 146–148.)

146

147

148

Variation: Perform an offensive front kick (with your rear leg) and then return your leg to its starting position. As you do so, perform a roundhouse kick with your forward leg. (See figures 149–151.)

Variation: You can perform both kicks with the same leg. Strike with the front kick using your forward leg. As you return your foot to the starting position, shift your body slightly and perform a roundhouse with the same foot. (See figures 152–154.)

Variation: Instead of striking with your forward leg, strike with your rear leg, then shift your body slightly as you return to the starting position and perform a roundhouse with the same foot. (See figures 155–156.)

 149 150

 151 152

 153 154

 155 156

Side kick-turn back-kick combination

As with the previous combination, you can use either the front leg or the rear leg to perform the side kick, but the front leg is faster. (Unlike the above combination, this combination cannot be performed with the same leg.)

157

1. Perform the side kick with your forward leg. Instead of returning your leg to the starting position, set it down in front of you and continue following your body's momentum as you make a complete revolution. Fire a turn back kick as soon as your back faces your opponent. Then continue the revolution and return to a fighter's stance. (See figures 157–161).

158

159

160

161

162

163

164

165

2. Perform the side kick with your rear leg. Instead of returning your leg to the starting position, set it down in front of you and continue following your body's momentum as you make a complete revolution. Fire a turn back kick as soon as your back faces your opponent. Then continue the revolution and return to a fighter's stance.

166

(See figures 162–166.) The faster you get your head turned back around to face your opponent, the more torque (power) this devastating kick produces.

167

168

169

Roundhouse kick-side kick combination

As with the front kick-roundhouse kick combination, you can use either the forward leg or the rear leg to launch the roundhouse kick, and then use the opposite leg for the side kick. Or, you can use the same leg to perform both kicks. This last option is the fastest.

1. Perform a roundhouse kick to your partner's head with your forward leg. This will bring her hands up to guard. Set your foot down and immediately perform a side kick with your rear leg. (See figures 167–169.)
2. Perform a roundhouse kick to your partner's head with your rear leg. Set your foot down and immediately perform a sidekick with your forward leg. (See figures 170–171.)
3. Perform a roundhouse kick with your forward leg. Set your foot down momentarily, then perform a sidekick with the same leg. (See figures 172–175.)
4. Perform a roundhouse kick to your partner's head with your rear leg. Set your foot down momentarily, then perform a side kick with the same leg. (See figures 175–176.)

Variation: You can also strike to the middle with the roundhouse kick, then follow with a side kick to the middle section.

KICK COMBINATIONS

 170

171

172

173

174

175

176

177

178

179

180

Low roundhouse kick-high roundhouse kick combination

Like the combinations described above, this combination can use your forward leg first, then your rear leg; or your rear leg first, then your forward leg; or the same leg for both kicks.

1. Perform a low roundhouse kick with your forward leg. As you return to the starting position, launch a high roundhouse kick with your rear leg. (See figures 178–180).
2. Perform a low roundhouse kick with your rear leg. As you return to the starting position, launch a high roundhouse kick with your forward leg. (See figures 181–183).
3. Perform a low roundhouse kick with your forward leg. Set your leg down momentarily, then launch a high roundhouse kick with the same leg. (See figures 184–185).
4. Perform a low roundhouse kick with your rear leg. Set your leg down momentarily, then launch a high roundhouse kick with the same leg. (See figures 186–187).

181

182

183

184

185

186

187

Variation: You can also reverse the order of the kicks and start with a high roundhouse kick, then a low roundhouse kick. Or you can perform one of the kicks to the middle section. Or you can perform the low round-house kick and the high roundhouse kick without setting your leg down between kicks.

Single kick volleys

It is also useful to send several volleys of the same kick (most common is the low round kick) to the same target. This can be totally incapacitating and is often used by Muay Thai kickboxers.

Vary the combinations

With all of these kicking combinations, you should move back and forth between variations. This confuses your opponent so she will not know what to expect next. For example, suppose you're using the low roundhouse-high roundhouse combination. Perform the first variation (low roundhouse kick with forward leg-high roundhouse kick with rear leg) several times in a row. The next time you perform a low round-house kick with your forward leg, your opponent will anticipate that you will perform a high roundhouse kick with your rear leg and may be ready to block, evade or counter-attack it. But this time, instead of following the forward leg roundhouse kick with a rear leg roundhouse kick, use the same leg (forward) to perform both roundhouse kicks. Your opponent will be blocking or evading to the wrong side and you can score your knockout kick.

Kicking combination drills

In order to get into the practice of combining kicks together, you should practice kicking drills with a partner.

Numbers game

Simply have your partner call out a number of kicks to perform (any number between two and six, for example). Then perform the specified number of kicks in a row.

Variation: With your partner, trade one kick combination apiece, one partner attacking and the other defending, then the defending partner becoming the attacker and the attacking partner defending. Then, have each partner do a two kick combination, then a three kick combination. This drill is especially helpful when you're transitioning into full contact sparring and would like to maintain some control over the sparring match.

Chase game

This requires extra room and no obstacles. With a partner, move back and forth in a straight line. Perform only kicking combinations as your partner backs away from you (she can also work on ducking, evading and blocking your techniques if so desired). Go the entire length of a room with one partner "chasing" the other, then switch sides and have the chased partner become the chaser. As you grow more skilled, go faster as you chase.

Hi-lo game

Have your partner call out a target area, such as low, middle or high, indicating that there's an opening. Perform a kicking combination that will take advantage of the open target area. With more experience, your partner can simply drop her guard instead of calling out a target area, and you respond by performing a kicking combination to take advantage of the dropped guard. As you grow more skilled, have your partner offer the dropped guard for shorter and shorter periods of time.

If you don't have a partner, practice the kick combinations against a heavy bag. One excellent drill is to practice sets of one drill for 2 or 3 minutes, then drop and do one minute of pushups. This helps build endurance to last during a round. It also builds strength!

FOR WOMEN ONLY: Women can use their flexibility to perform roundhouse kicks to the head, which can be a knockout technique in competition. To take advantage of this flexibility, practice by playing the "headhunter game" with a partner. Whoever scores the first unblocked kick to the head wins the game. To practice your combinations of kicks, add an additional incentive: if one person scores five unblocked kicks to any other target area, she wins. This will help both partners remember to use combinations and to guard both body and head.

FOR WOMEN ONLY: Many women are intimidated by the idea of physical contact when they first start training in kickboxing. Not only are women sometimes afraid of getting hurt, but they've been taught never to hurt other people. Because of this conditioning, use progressive contact conditioning to get used to sparring. Begin by practicing kicking combinations with a partner using no contact. Then, use light contact while strictly controlling conditions (each partner does only one kick combination, for example). Then, as your confidence grows, begin making more contact with your partner. Always remember to get your partner's approval before your step up the contact!

DEBZ SAYS: Wear your sparring equipment when you practice drills like this with a partner. It stinks to have to get your teeth replaced or your jaw repaired just because you were trying to prove how brave and tough you are!

11
PUNCH COMBINATIONS

Just as learning to use kicks in combination helps you become an unbeatable fighter, so too does learning to use punch combinations. Your opponent can probably block one punch pretty easily, but not three or four in a row. Just as with kicking, keeping your punches coming can overwhelm your opponent so that she does not counter-attack. As with kicking combinations, some punches work better together than others do. A jab followed by a spinning backfist works a bit better than a cross followed by a spinning backfist. Some combinations suggested below will help you practice, but experience should also be your guide: some will come more naturally to you and will be more effective for you than others.

Trainers sometimes number the punches so that they can call out combinations of punches for you to use. Instead of calling out "Jab, then cross, then hook," a trainer will say, "1, 2, 3." It helps if you know which numbers stand for which punches.

1 = jab
2 = cross
3 = hook
4 = uppercut
5 = overhand
6 = spinning backfist

This numbering system is behind that old saying, "Give him the old one-two." What this really means is, "Give him the old jab-cross punching combination." But "Give him the old one-two" sounds better.

To memorize the numbering system (if your trainer uses it), simply have a partner call out numbers while you hit the heavy bag. She should correct you if you use the wrong technique.

It is easiest to practice these combinations on a heavy bag at first, but as you grow more confident, you should practice with a partner. This allows you to account for unexpected moves, blocks that shove you out of position and counter-attacks you weren't ready for. You can also use shadow boxing (use a mirror) to get a feel for how punching combinations should flow. Your punches should move in reciprocal motion. As you snap back one punch, you should be firing the other so that by the time your first hand returns to your jaw, your second hand has landed. Now your first hand is ready to fire again. Unlike the kicking combinations, you rarely use the same hand to deliver more than one punch in a row. The exception is the jab, which you may throw several time in order to feel your opponent out and to wait for the opportune moment to throw a cross. With all other punches, it's better to simply alternate arms. Even if, for example, you simply use the cross over and over, you should alternate arms in order to take advantage of your body movement and to increase your punching speed. It takes longer to use the same hand to punch twice in a row than it does to alternate hands. Try it on the heavy bag sometime. Alternating hands also provides a constant guard from the non-punching hand. Remember to use the power of your entire body, pivoting from the foot, knee, hip and core to fire each punch. Visualize that punch exploding all the way through the target.

Jab-cross combination

The jab-cross combination is the heart of punching. Most combinations build on this one, so start here. You can jab more than one time in order to feel your opponent out and to vary the rhythm, but follow up with a cross. Work on this combination until it comes naturally. Alternate your forward leg and jabbing hand in order to build even balance as a fighter. (See figures 189 - 190.)

189   190

Jab-cross-hook combination

Once you've mastered the jab-cross, start adding other punches to your combinations. Perform a jab with your forward arm. As you return the jab to its starting position, launch the cross with your rear hand. As you return the cross to its starting position, launch the hook with your forward hand. (See figures 191–193.)

191

192

193

Jab-uppercut

To vary your combinations and to confuse your opponent, try the jab-uppercut. Your opponent will be expecting a jab-cross, and the uppercut might be able to slide through her defenses. Perform the jab with your forward arm, then as you return the jab to its starting position, launch the uppercut. (See figures 194–195.)

Jab-spinning backfist

Just like the jab-uppercut can confuse your opponent, the jab-spinning backfist will be totally unexpected. Perform the jab with your forward hand. As you pivot into the punch, continue pivoting and perform the spinning backfist with your other hand. (See figures 196–197.)

Jab-overhand

Use this combination against the opponent who is expecting a jab-cross. Use the overhand to get through her defenses. (See figures 198–199.)

194

195

196

197

198

199

Remember, you can devise your own punching combinations, too. In fact, this will help vary your sparring and keep you unpredictable. (And predictable fighters never win matches. Well, hardly ever.) For instance, you can add punches to any of the above combinations. The jab-cross-hook could become the jab-cross-hook-spinning backfist, if that works for you.

As with kicking combinations, vary the punching combinations you use against an opponent in order to confuse her. Set her up. For example, perform the jab-cross combination several times in a row. The next time you perform a jab, she'll be expecting you to follow it with a cross. Instead, perform an uppercut.

FOR WOMEN ONLY: Since women tend to think of their upper bodies as weak, especially as compared to their lower bodies, they often overlook the advantages of punches. This is a mistake. You can throw a lot more punches than you can kicks before you get tired. You can target more accurately with punches. And you can use punches in closer, which helps if you're at a height disadvantage (your legs won't reach your opponent but her legs reach you). Since kicks do more damage than punches, you're better off in punching range even if your opponent's reach is longer than yours, especially if you're clever and overwhelm her with combinations of punches.

FOR WOMEN ONLY: You may not be able to deliver a knockout punch (lighter weight fighters rarely do) but you can disorient your opponent by delivering combinations of punches in quick succession. This might leave her open for a powerful roundhouse kick. After a series of punches, she may not even be expecting a kick—and bam! You win the match.

DEBZ SAYS: A key to success in kickboxing is building strength and endurance, especially if a woman feels she has an upper body disadvantage. Why not be one of the still relatively small group of women competitors who train the upper body hard, thereby gaining an edge over most opponents? Most females don't realize how absolutely beautiful a cut and toned upper body is on a woman!

12
KICK-PUNCH COMBINATIONS

Of course, you're training to be a kickboxer, not a kicker OR a boxer, so you want to use your kicking and punching techniques *together*. This can be difficult to do since you need to be in closer to punch than you do to kick. Many beginning fighters will perform kicking and punching combinations from kicking range, which means their punches have no hope of landing on the opponent. The opponent can ignore the punches. All that wasted energy just wears you out ! In order to perform kick-punch combinations effectively, you must always be aware of your range. This, of course, varies from person to person, depending on the length of your arms and legs. With practice you should be able to judge how close you need to be in order to land that cross or that roundhouse kick. As you perform kick-punch combinations, you will have to use footwork and foot placement to move into and out of the appropriate fighting ranges.

Suggested kick-punch combinations follow, but you will want to make up your own as well. Again, you'll be able to perform some combinations more naturally than others, and you may prefer to do certain kicks. Remember to mix it up, using kicks and punches, front leg kicks and rear leg kicks, low kicks, middle kicks and high kicks, and middle and high punches. Consider how well the techniques flow together. You don't want choppy, start-and-stop combinations. These are inefficient and slow. Instead, practice different techniques together to see how you can move easily from one technique to the next. Also, don't simply rely on two techniques in a row to get the job done. Think of three or four (or more) technique combinations. This helps you confuse and overwhelm your opponent. And if the first two or three techniques don't score, the next two or three might. This is where possessing super endurance is critical! Using all those large muscle groups together for any extended period of time is totally fatiguing. To paraphrase an old adage, "The last WOMAN standing usually wins!" To learn more about conditioning for endurance, see Chapter 13.

200

201

Jab-roundhouse combination

Perform a jab with your forward arm. As you return the arm to its starting position, turn your body and perform a rear leg roundhouse kick. (See figures 200–201.)

Variation: Consider adding more punches: try a jab-cross-hook-roundhouse combination, or a jab-cross-uppercut-roundhouse.

Variation: Perform a jab, then a front leg (defensive) roundhouse kick.

Jab-cross-rear knee strike

Perform a jab with your forward hand. Then perform a cross with your rear hand. Instead of returning your hands to their starting positions, grab the opponent and deliver a rear knee strike. (See figures 202 – 205.)

Variation: Consider adding more punches: try a jab-cross-hook-uppercut-rear knee strike. Or try different punches, such as jab-uppercut-rear knee strike.

202

203

204

205

Front kick-jab-cross

In this combination, you start in kicking range, then move into punching range. To do this, perform a front kick with your forward leg. Then set your leg down in front of you rather than returning it to its rear position. Don't lean forward or overbalance yourself to do this. As your kick lands, fire a jab with your forward hand, then a cross with your rear hand. (See figures 206–208.)

Variation: You can perform this combination using your front leg to do the front kick, and simply set the leg down in front of you, then perform the punches.

206

207

208

Variation: You can add more punches after the cross.

Variation: You can use the front kick-roundhouse kick combination to set up the punches.

Variation: Perform the combination backwards: do the punches as described, then push the opponent back with a front kick.

Side kick-jab-cross

In this combination, start in kicking range, then move into punching range, as above. Perform a sidekick with your rear leg. Set your leg down in front of you rather than returning it to its rear position. As your kick lands, jab with your forward hand, then perform a cross with your rear hand. (See figures 209–211.)

209

Variations: The same variations can be used as were used for the front kick-jab-cross. Use your front leg instead of your rear leg to perform the side kick. Add more punches after the cross. Use the side kick-turn kick combination to set up the punches.

210
211

Roundhouse kick-jab-cross-roundhouse kick combination

Perform a front leg roundhouse kick. As you set your foot down in front of you, jab with your forward hand, then add a cross with your rear hand. As you return your rear hand to its starting position, perform a roundhouse kick with your rear leg. This is a devastating combination and a great "finisher!" (See figures 212–215.)

212

213

214

215

Vary these combinations to create some of your own. For instance, try using a rear leg front kick instead of a rear leg roundhouse kick in the previous combination (thereby getting roundhouse kick-jab-cross-front kick). Or insert additional punches or kicks that work with the way your body moves. To think of additional combinations, practice the kicking combinations as described in Chapter 10, adding some punches to the end (or at the beginning or in the middle). Then practice the punching combinations as described in Chapter 11, adding kicks to the beginning, middle or end. Can you imagine a jab-spinning backfist-roundhouse kick combination? Why not try it out?

Work with a partner to refine combinations that work for you. The partner can help you determine whether your combinations are effective and can help you tweak them for maximum damage.

FOR WOMEN ONLY: Sometimes women who take up kickboxing have never seen an actual boxing or kickboxing fight. It is difficult to imagine how combinations are used if you haven't watched other people fight in the ring. Although you need personal experience, invest some time and energy into becoming a spectator, too. Watch and critique fights on television. If kickboxing or similar tournaments are being held nearby, make an effort to attend and analyze what the fighters are doing. What techniques seem most effective? How do the fighters move in the ring? Rent videos, watch cable television and see live events to understand how fighters fight.

FOR WOMEN ONLY: Although you'll only fight real kickboxing matches against women, be sure to have some male sparring partners. Clearly define a set of rules—how hard to kick and punch, for example—so that you don't get hurt, but don't spar only women. This is especially important if you want to use kickboxing techniques in self-defense situations.

DEBZ SAYS: Kickboxing is still in its relative infancy with regard to female competition. Most trainers and coaches are men. Sparring and training with men can build a woman's confidence and strength, so this is not bad. But it would be nice to see more women trainers and coaches. Could you be one? If you get a chance to be a role model for other female kickboxers, give it your best effort. True competitors always give back to their sport.

13
CONDITIONING, FLEXIBILITY AND WEIGHT TRAINING

In addition to simply learning and practicing kickboxing techniques, a good kickboxer must work on conditioning, flexibility and weight training. Some of this work can be incorporated in the kickboxing workout, but you may need to do additional work, such as weight training, on the side. Some of the drills and exercises here can be done at various times throughout the day without necessarily changing into workout clothes and hitting the gym. For example, some of the flexibility exercises can be done while you're sitting on the floor watching television or grading papers. Weight training can take the form of lifting more things at home. Conditioning can include parking your car farther from the mall entrance and walking briskly whenever possible, rather than using a leisurely stroll to get from on place to another. How about taking the stairs in lieu of the elevator, raking leaves instead of using a leaf blower, and getting up off the couch to switch TV stations instead of using the remote control? Small changes accumulate and turn into visible changes!

Although women tend to be more flexible than men, you may need to work on your flexibility in order to perform the techniques of kickboxing, such as high roundhouse kicks. In addition, if you begin weight training, you need to counteract the effects of building your muscles by keeping them stretched. (Think of the term "muscle-bound bully." The idea that a bulked up person can't move very fast has some basis in reality. This potential problem can be solved by faithfully doing flexibility exercises and stretches every day as often as possible).

A number of stretching exercises can improve flexibility, including those described earlier. The following flexibility exercises will also improve your ability to kick and will increase your ability to perform everyday tasks.

Side bend

Standing up straight, tilt your upper body to the side, reaching over the top of your head with the opposite arm. Stretch as far as you can and hold for 15 seconds. Repeat on both sides 10 times. (See figure 216.)

216

Hip rotation

Place your palm against a wall for support, if needed. Bend your knee and rotate your leg in a circle, moving your leg from the front to the side, then reversing direction. Repeat this rotation five times for each leg. (See figures 217–218.)

217

218

Calf stretch

Place your palms against a wall, about shoulders-width apart. Bend your elbows slightly. Extend one leg behind you until your toes just touch the ground. Press down with your heel, stretching the calf muscle. Hold 10 seconds, then relax and repeat five times on each leg. (See figures 219–220).

219

220

Body bridge

On your back, bend your knees so that you feet rest flat on the floor. Place your palms flat on the floor next to your ears. Arch your back, tilting your hips toward the ceiling. Hold the position for 15 seconds. Return to the start position and repeat five times. (See figures 221–222).

221

222

Groin lift

Stand with your side against a wall or hold onto a chair back. Perform a sidekick slowly. Hold your leg in the extended position for 15 seconds, then relax and repeat with the other leg. Do five lifts with each leg, trying to kick and hold your leg higher with each attempt. To achieve a better stretch, have a partner hold your extended leg and push up until you can feel the stretch. Hold this position while your partner slowly releases your leg. Don't let your leg drop, but hold it in this position for 15 seconds. (See figures 223–225).

223

224

225

Hamstring lift

Stand with your back against the wall for support. Perform a front kick. Keep your leg extended. Hold this position for 15 seconds. Then relax and repeat with the other leg. Do five lifts with each leg, trying to hold your leg higher with each attempt. For a better stretch, have a partner hold your extended leg and push up until you can feel the stretch. Hold the position while your partner slowly releases your leg. Don't let

226

227

228

your leg drop, but hold it in this position for 15 seconds. (See figures 226–228).

In addition, you can use the stretches described in Chapter Four to increase flexibility. When possible, perform these flexibility exercises in a dry sauna or in a pool. The warmth of the sauna keeps the muscles pliable and allows more freedom of movement. The pool allows the stretches to be done in slow motion against resistance, which gently builds strength as well as flexibility.

To quickly improve your flexibility, incorporate flexibility exercises into your daily schedule. For example, at work, perhaps you can perform hip rotations or side bends or calf stretches. Especially if you work in front of a computer monitor or at a desk most of the time, work in neck, shoulder, wrist and ankle stretches. In the morning, read the newspaper on the floor while doing an open stretch. Perform hip stretches while watching your favorite television show. By adding these routines to your daily activities, you will gain much more flexibility than if you limit your exercises to a specific workout time. You may also find that these flexibility exercises will help relieve tension and stress throughout the day and give you small, needed breaks.

Increasing speed

The most important mathematical equation for kickboxers to know is this: speed times mass equals power. This means a small person can be as powerful as a large person—as long as the small person is very, very fast. Speed translates into power, which makes it an essential component of kickboxing. Women, who already have the advantage of speed, can enhance their abilities with the following drills.

Although it seems hard to believe, you achieve speed through relaxing. The more relaxed you are, the quicker you are. To prove the point, try this: with your right arm chambered at your jaw, make a tight fist. Clench your arm muscles as tightly as possible. Now punch forward as hard as you can. Next, relax your arm muscles. Shake the tightness out. Make a loose fist, chambering your hand in a relaxed position near your jaw. Now punch forward.

Makes a lot of difference, doesn't it? The second technique is much faster than the first. Of course, the second technique can become sloppy and less powerful if you're not careful. To prevent this, tighten your muscles at the moment of impact. This creates a quick and powerful technique.

Clench-and-release exercise

Clench all of your arm muscles as tightly as possible. Hold this clenched position for about 15 seconds. Then, shake your arm loose, relaxing as much as you can. Repeat this process several times with both arms. Through this practice, you'll learn what a relaxed muscle feels like, and you'll more easily relax before performing your techniques.

Creating whip-like movements

Adding a snapping or whipping movement to the end of each technique increases the speed and force of your techniques. For example, if you punch and land your punch solidly, you will have a strong technique. However, the power of the punch will only come from the pushing motion that you have performed. You've eliminated the speed of the technique and so have reduced the power of it. On the other hand, if you punch, and, after landing your punch, pull your punch back quickly, you create a snap at the end of your punch. This adds speed to your technique, making it sting.

Try this: using a punching bag or target, punch as hard as you can, landing your punch solidly. Stop your punch when you reach your target. Then, punch as hard as you can, pulling your punch back to the starting position after it has reached the target, moving as quickly as you can. You should see a definite difference in speed and snap.

Practice adding this snap or whip to the end of a technique by returning your hand or foot to its starting position (the chamber position) as soon as your strike has reached its target.

Punching drill

Use a target such as a heavy bag. Stand far enough away from the target that you can barely touch it when you straighten your arm fully. Punch the target using different punching techniques. Move as quickly as possible. Return your hand to the chamber position as fast as you punch out with it, increasing your speed as you practice. Use good technique. Begin by striking 60 times per half-minutes. Build up from there. Remember to train both sides.

229

Slipping drill

Work with a partner for this drill. Your partner should strike using different techniques. Keeping your feet planted, pivot at the waist and turn your upper body away from the strikes. As you grow proficient, have your partner increase her striking speed and vary the height and location of her strikes. Wait until your partner actually launches the strikes. Then, shift out of the way as quickly as possible. Work in two-minute increments. (See figure 229.)

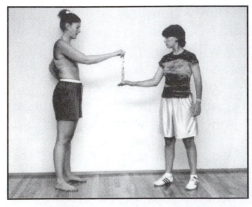

230

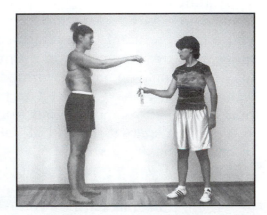

231

Hand reaction time drill

Work with a partner to perform this drill. You'll also need a ruler. Have your partner place the "zero" end of the ruler between your thumb and forefinger. Your thumb and finger should remain about an inch apart. When your partner lets go of the ruler (at random), pinch it between your thumb and finger as quickly as possible. Don't move your hand up or down, simply close your thumb and finger together. Note the measurement on the ruler where you caught it. Practice until you can catch the ruler within the first inch or two. (See figures 230–231.)

Foot reaction time drill

Have your partner hold a target in front of you. Assume a fighting stance position. When your partner says "go" (at random), kick the target using any technique. Practice until you can hit the target immediately after hearing the signal.

Foot reaction drill

You'll need a partner and a piece of paper for this drill. The partner should hold the piece of paper at shoulder height, a few feet away from you but within kicking range. When your partner lets go of the paper (at random), strike it with a kicking technique before it touches the ground or floats out of range. Since the paper doesn't fall directly to the ground, you must make adjustments in your kick to strike it. (See figures 232–233).

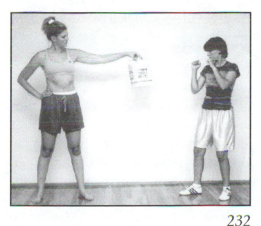

232   233

If ducking, slipping and other evasion techniques seem beyond your abilities, you may need plyometric drills. These drills help you gain explosive power and explosive movements, which means improved agility and response time, too. The games you played as a kid are great for building plyometric speed: hopscotch, jump rope and the like can all help you increase your speed and agility. Try the following exercises as well.

Warning: These plyometric drills require strong knees. Avoid them if you have knee problems or are concerned with your knee strength. If you haven't been working out regularly, skip these until you have a strong foundation of rock-hard quadriceps and flexible joints. If in doubt, consult your trainer or physician.

Frog jumps

234

Squat on the floor, keeping your hands out for balance. Leap from your way across the room as quickly as possible. Keep up continual leapfrogging for 30 seconds, adding on five seconds at a time. When you can do 60 leapfrogs in 60 seconds, you'll have improved your speed considerably.

Variation: Have a partner use a blocking target or any long, flexible object to sweep at your feet so that you must jump up to avoid hitting the target. Your partner should sweep back and forth quickly, without allowing pauses between jumps. Your partner can increase the height at which he or she sweeps (aiming at the knees eventually) as you improve. (See figure 234.)

Jumping drill

235

Stack cushions or pillows on the floor, starting with a height of about eight inches. Jump from one side of the stack to the other as quickly as you can without stopping and without knocking the cushions over. Stack the cushions higher as you improve. When you are able to stack the cushions as high as your knees and complete 15 jumps in thirty seconds, you'll have increased your speed considerably. (See figure 235.)

Power drills

Although speed can increase power, strength or mass is the other necessary element of power, and getting it requires equal dedication. Strength can be gained through a variety of means, including repetition of techniques and weight lifting.

Although women can rely on speed to give them some advantage in kickboxing, you should also build strength. The two combined equal power. While a fast strike with nothing behind it might sting and a powerful strike with no speed might bruise, only the combination of speed and strength can create a devastating impact.

Isometric/isotonic exercises

Exercises that require you to lift your own body weight are excellent for building strength. These include crunches, pull-ups and push-ups. And since they require little or no equipment, they're very cost-effective.

Crunches

Crunches work your abdominal muscles. Although situps were once recommended for strengthening this area of the body, they are now considered too dangerous to do—they're very hard on your back and usually work your hip flexors more than your abs.

Lie on the floor, knees bent, feet on the floor. Put your hands behind your ears. Don't put your hands under your neck or lace your fingers together; this creates too much strain on your neck. Using only your abdominal muscles, roll forward so that your shoulders lift off the ground. It takes a lot of mental concentration to train your abs well, so focus on the muscles being used at all phases of the exercise. Look straight up throughout the exercise, as this will alleviate neck strain. Pull your navel

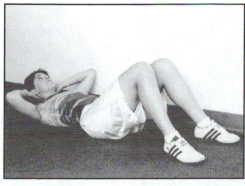

236

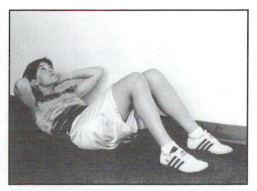

237

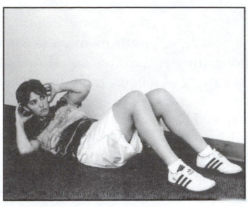
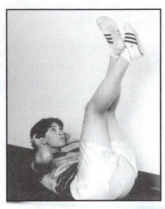

238   239

in toward your spine and push your spine into the floor. Moving slowly and deliberately, return to your starting position. You need to move slowly and smoothly to avoid using momentum instead of muscles to do the work. Keep your neck and jaws relaxed at all times. Repeat the crunch 15 times. (See figures 236–237.)

Variations:

1. Twist to the right as you crunch, by leading with your left shoulder, NOT your elbow (a common mistake). Then twist to the left by leading with your right shoulder. This type of crunch works your oblique abdominal muscles which are otherwise hard to tone. As before, always look up and relax your neck. (See figure 238.)

2. Cross your legs and lift them at a 90 degree angle to the floor. Perform each crunch in this position. (See figure 239.)

Boxer situps

Work with a partner. Lie on your back, with your head slightly between the feet of your partner, who should be standing. Grasp your

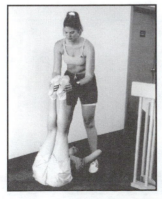

240   241   242

partner's ankles and raise your legs 90 degrees. Have your partner push your legs down forcefully. Don't let them touch the ground. Lift your legs back up and have your partner push them down again. Work as quickly as possible. Repeat 15 times.

As a variation, have your partner push your legs to the right or the left instead of straight down. (See figures 240–242.)

Push-ups

Start with basic push-ups and build from there. To perform a basic push-up, rest on the floor with your palms directly under your shoulders. Feet together, place your toes on the floor so that your body weight rests on your toes and your palms. Tighten your abdomen and straighten your back and shoulders. From this position, push directly up. Fully extend your arms but don't lock your elbows out. Move smoothly and evenly. Going too fast can put too much strain on your elbows, especially in the beginning when your body may not be accustomed to the effort. (See figures 243–244.)

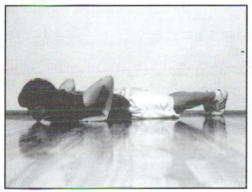

243

244

245

246

247 248

If the basic push-up position is too difficult to do at first (or your abdominal muscles need pampering, such as after childbirth or a hysterectomy), keep your knees on the floor. Although this reduces the amount of body weight your arms lift and thus reduces the resistance and the effectiveness of the exercise, it does isolate the arm muscles, making them do all the work, so it serves as a reasonable substitute. (See figures 245–246.)

249

Start with three sets of 15 push-ups each. While your goal will change over time, aim for 75 pushups in a row resting only on your palms and toes.

In order to strengthen different muscles in your arms and upper body, simply vary the position of your hands as you do pushups. If you spread your hands so that your palms rest two shoulders' width apart (instead of directly under your shoulders), you will work your chest muscles more. (See figure 247.)

If you bring your hands close together under your sternum, you will work your triceps more. (Be careful of this variation if you have elbow trouble, such as tendinitis.) (See figure 248.)

Finally, if you use that old martial arts standby, the knuckle pushup, you will strengthen your wrists and forearms, leading to stronger, more correct, punching techniques. You perform a knuckle pushup by resting your weight on the two punching knuckles of each fist (instead of resting your weight on your open palms.) (See figure 249.)

250

251

252

253

Pull-ups

If you have access to a pull-up bar (kits that attach to a doorway can be purchased inexpensively for home use), work on pull-ups. This is one of the most effective ways to strengthen your arms and lats without investing in weight equipment and without spending a lot of time in the weight room. A pull-up is simple to do. Standing straight, with your feet comfortably apart, grasp the bar with your palms facing away from you, your hands in line with your shoulders. Pull yourself up from the floor. The goal is to get your chin above the bar. If you cannot do even one or two pull-ups at first (many women can't), don't feel embarrassed and give up. Instead, enlist a friend to act as spotter. The spotter will help

254

you lift your weight. Some more complicated pieces of fitness equipment allow you to practice pull-ups without a spotter; instead of lifting your entire body weight, you specify the amount of weight you will pull up and the machine does the rest.

To strengthen other muscles in your arms, change your grip on the bar. For instance, if you grip so that your palms face you, you'll work your biceps more (if you grip facing away, you use more of your triceps). You can grip the bar with your hands close together or with your hands spread far apart. All of these variations increase your overall muscle strength by training and building all of the muscles in your arms and shoulders. (See figures 250–254.)

Flutter kicks

These build abdominal strength. Lie on your back with a towel under the small of your back and your arms folded under your head. Lift your legs and "flutter" them as if you were swimming. Do a 15 second interval, then rest and repeat. (See figure 255.)

Scissor kicks

On your back, place your hands (or a towel) under the small of your back for support. Lift your legs off the floor and move them together and apart, as if your legs were a pair of scissors. Begin with 15 second intervals, building up to 30 second intervals. (See figure 256).

255

256

Leg lifts

Once you can do scissor kicks easily, move onto leg lifts. (Don't perform leg lifts if you have back problems). Lie on your back and place your hands under the small of your back for support. Lift both legs six inches off the floor. Hold for 10 seconds. Without letting your feet touch the floor, raise your legs to 12 inches. Hold for 10 seconds. Increase in six-inch increments until

257

your legs reach a 90 degree angle to the floor. Then slowly lower your legs in six-inch increments, holding for 10 seconds at each level. (See figure 257).

Rope ups

These also build abdominal strength and should only be done when you can do leg lifts. Don't perform rope ups if you have back problems. Lie on your back, placing your hands under the small of your back for support. Lift your legs so they form a 90 degree angle with your body. Imagine a rope extending from the ceiling attached to your ankles. Roll your hips upward so that your extended legs rise several inches toward the ceiling, as if the imaginary rope were pulling them up. Hold for 10 seconds and repeat 10 times. (See figures 258–259.)

Strength through techniques practice

Practicing kicks and punches full power is one way to increase strength. You'll need a heavy bag to do this, or a strong partner with a

258

259

kicking target. Your goal should be to knock the heavy bag (or your partner) back at least several inches with every technique. Practice techniques in a continual motion for two minute rounds for the best workout.

If you don't have access to a heavy bag or a cooperative partner, you can still build strength through practicing martial arts techniques by slow motion kicking. (This is a great drill even if you do have a partner and a heavy bag.)

Begin by practicing your techniques slowly in front of a mirror. Although you can practice hand techniques in slow motion, the real strength building comes when you practice kicks slowly. Use this time to perfect your techniques, as well. Look at your chamber in the mirror. Is it high? Is it tight? Is your body in the correct position? As you get the hang of kicking slowly (it requires balance), slow down your kicks until you're practicing in slow motion. Gradually increase the amount of time it takes for you to do each kick. Aim for a goal of spending an entire 60 seconds on one technique. Practice each of your kicks on each of your legs 10 times for an excellent strength building workout. You can perform slow motion kicks in the swimming pool for added resistance training.

Strength training

Lifting weights to build strength can improve many aspects of your kickboxing training. While practicing kickboxing techniques and performing body conditioning exercises will give you strength, weight training can fill in any gaps and can help you quickly improve areas in drastic need of attention. For instance, if your upper body strength is minimal, you may need to lift weights to make serious progress, since there is a limit to how much strength you can build doing pushups and practicing hand strikes against a heavy bag.

Weight training basics

You build strength and muscle through resistance training, which is what weight lifting is. You can provide resistance with free weights, such as barbells and dumbbells. Free weights consist of metal bars with weighted plates attached to each end. Dumbbells are small, meant to be lifted with one hand. Barbells are longer, meant to be lifted with both hands.

You can also use weight machines, which have a stack of weight plates permanently set in place. You simply select the weight you want to use, then lift the weights by lifting or pushing on a bar or a set of handles.

Free weights have certain advantages. Because your muscles must balance the weights, you work the smaller, stabilizer muscles that can be difficult to strengthen otherwise. Free weights require equal strength on both sides of your body. When you lift a barbell, your left arm must work as hard as your right arm to keep the bar straight. A stronger arm can't compensate for a weaker one, as can happen with weight machines.

Weight machines have advantages as well. They're safer to use. (You're not going to drop a weight machine on your foot.) You don't need a spotter as frequently. Weight machines don't require a lot of experience to use, so you're more likely to use them correctly. Also, you can isolate and work on just one muscle at a time on a weight machine. This way, you actually work your biceps instead of your shoulder or vice versa. Finally, since the weights on a weight machine are easy to change, your workout can go faster and more smoothly.

Which you use depends largely on which you have access to. In some ways, the best approach is to use both free weights and machine weights.

Getting started

Two words often thrown around in gyms are *rep* and *set*. The word *rep* is short for *repetition*, and it simply means a doing a single exercise one time. Therefore, one rep means doing an exercise one time. Two reps means twice, and so on. The word *set* refers to the group of repetitions you do for any exercise. For example, if you do 10 repetitions of one exercise before resting, your set consists of 10 reps. If you rest for a minute and then do 10 more of the same exercise before moving on to the next, you've just done two sets of 10 reps each. The number of reps or sets you do is related to your strength training goals.

When you start lifting, you should have an idea of your goals in order to plan your overall weight training strategy. If you want to add a lot of muscle bulk, your plan should be different from someone who simply wants a more toned body. Most women want to become stronger and more defined without bulking up.

Whenever you lift weights, you actually create microscopic tears in the muscle fibers in the targeted area. As those muscle fibers heal, they become thicker and stronger. Therefore, the more weight you lift, the thicker and stronger your muscles grow. If you lift less weight for more repetitions, you'll still stimulate muscle teardown and regrowth, but it won't be as obvious. That's why many women choose this option: lifting less weight equals toned but not bulky muscles.

Generally, toning and defining muscles requires between 8 and 15 repetitions of each exercise in one or two sets. Two sets of 10 to 12 repetitions is ideal for beginners. Once you've been lifting for a while, you should move onto three sets. You should lift enough weight so that you have difficulty completing that last repetition. As you grow stronger, you'll add additional weight so that the last repetition always remains a challenge to complete. A program that follows these guidelines improves muscle endurance, which means your muscles can perform difficult tasks for longer periods of time. For a kickboxer, muscle endurance is as important as stamina or cardiovascular fitness (maybe even more important).

To produce a stronger, more muscular look, limit your repetitions to between five and nine (six is ideal). Again, your last repetition should be very difficult to do; therefore, you're lifting a much heavier weight than if you were doing 10 or 12 repetitions. However, lifting heavier weights fewer times doesn't increase your muscle endurance, so unless a really powerful body is your goal, most kickboxers should aim for the 10-to-12 rep range.

Lifting weights correctly

Each repetition of an exercise should be done smoothly and evenly without bouncing or jerking. It should take about the same amount of time to lift the weight as to lower it. Don't pause between lifting and lowering the weight; this can be very stressful on your joints. Take about four or five seconds to perform each exercise.

Breathe correctly with each repetition. Untrained lifters often hold their breath as they perform their exercises. This is very dangerous, since it can cause a spike in blood pressure, which is hard on the heart.

Exhale during the lift itself. Inhale during the lowering part of the exercise. Concentrate on your breathing to find a good, even rhythm for your exercises. After each set, you should rest from 30 to 60 seconds to recover. Active rest is best. Rather than just sitting there panting like so many you see in the gym, keep moving by stretching the muscles just worked. This pumps more blood into the exercised area and hastens the waste removal process (which lessens post-exercise soreness). This "pump" of blood is what really helps muscles grow and become stronger and is the much sought-after effect so commonly desired by bodybuilders.

Lifting frequency

When you start lifting weights, you want to see immediate results. But if you hit the gym every day, don't be surprised if you don't make any progress and end up with an injury. Remember, you're tearing down your muscles, so they need time to heal. Never lift with the same set of muscles two days in a row. Unlike aerobic workouts, you don't need to lift every day to get and maintain a good set of muscles. You should lift at least twice a week (or you'll lose ground), but even then your workout can be a quick run through. You can easily combine weight training with your martial arts workout without taking too much time away from the rest of your life.

Recent research shows that the best approach is to give each body part several days' rest between lifting sessions. The ideal is to work only your upper or your lower body in each weight lifting session, and to give yourself a day off between each session. Thus, for Week One, you might do upper body on Monday, lower body on Wednesday, then upper body again on Friday. On Tuesday, Thursday, and Saturday, you would do cardio training or kickboxing training. You take Sunday off (you deserve it!). When you start again the following Monday, you simply reverse the previous week's training. Week Two, would have you doing lower body on Monday, upper body on Wednesday and lower body again on Friday, of course doing cardio or kickboxing training on Tuesday, Thursday and Saturday. Week Three's schedule would be the same as Week One's. This approach allows at least three days' rest for each body part. It has been shown that more intensive weight training is actually counter-productive.

Chest press/bench press

This exercise works the chest, triceps and the front of the shoulder. Using free weights, this exercise is called the bench press. A barbell is usually used, but dumbbells (one in each hand) can also be used. Rest on the bench with your feet flat on the floor. If you're short, place a step or block (found in most gyms) at the end of the bench to place your feet on so your back doesn't arch. Grip the bar so that your hands are about shoulder-width apart. Lift the bar straight up in line with your shoulders, straightening your arms. Move slowly and smoothly. Lower the bar until your elbows dip slightly below the plane of the bench. Push the bar back up to repeat the exercise. Use a spotter if you're using a barbell. (See figures 260–264.)

On a weight machine, this exercise is called the chest press. Adjust the seat so that you can grip the handles comfortably, without arching your back. Start with your elbows bent, then push up on the handles, breathing out as you exert yourself. (See figures 265–266.)

Many different weight machines have the same name or perform a similar function. It's best to read the instructions attached to each machine (or get advice from the gym staff) before trying them out. Some

260

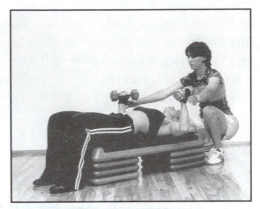

261

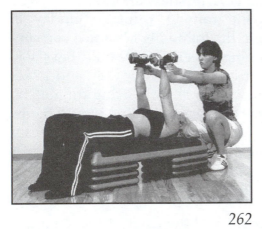

262

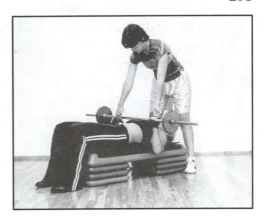

263

264

265   266

machines work better than others for particular body types. One machine may fit a taller person better than a shorter person. When you use weight machines, always adjust the seat and other variables to fit you most comfortably.

Butterfly press/bench fly

This exercise works the chest, the shoulders and the biceps. It is called the bench fly when it is done with free weights. Use a pair of dumbbells. Rest on the bench, with your feet flat on the floor. Don't let your back arch. Start with your arms to the sides, your elbows just past the plane of the bench. Keeping your elbows slightly bent, lift your arms back toward each other, squeezing the chest muscles (pectorals). Then lower your arms until your elbows move just past the plane of the bench and repeat. (See figures 267–268.)

Using a weight machine, this exercise is called the butterfly press. Sitting in the seat, reach behind you and place your palms and forearms flat against the padded handles. Squeeze your arms toward each other, trying to touch your palms together across your chest. When your hands are a few inches apart, spread your arms to lower the weight. (See figures 269–270.)

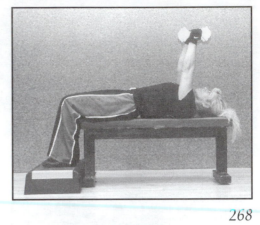

267

268

269

270

271

272

Lateral pull down

This exercise works the laterals, the muscles that run along the side of the chest and the back. It also works the shoulders and biceps. This exercise is usually done with a machine. Stand and grab the handle above you. Sit down, gripping the handles with your arms straight. Now you're ready to begin the exercise. This is one of the few exercises where you really need to have a small arch in the lower back and, as always, pull your abs in toward your spine. For this exercise, inhale as the handles go up and exhale as you pull down toward the chest.

Pull the handles straight down until they are even with your chest, then slowly extend your arms straight up. Do not lean back. This common mistake places undue stress on delicate shoulder and neck muscles. When you're finished with your set, stand up, then release the handle, allowing the weight stack to return to its position. (See figures 271–272.)

Lateral raise

The exercise works the laterals and the shoulder muscles. It is usually done with free weights. Use a pair of dumbbells. Hold them at your sides, keeping your elbows slightly bent. Slowly swing your arms out to the sides and up to about shoulder height. Then move your arms back down to the starting position. (See figures 273–274.)

Standard biceps curl

Standing or sitting as you hold dumbbells at your side, palms facing in, raise them in front of your body as palms face upward. Squeeze your

273

274

275   276

277   278

biceps at the top of the movement, then slowly return to the starting position. (See figures 275–276.)

To use a barbell, grip the bar so that it rests on the top of your thighs. Your hands should be about shoulder-width apart. Bend both arms so the bar curls up, not quite touching your chest. Then straighten your arms so that the bar returns to its position near your thighs. (See figures 277–278.)

Biceps concentration curl

To perform with dumbbells, sit with your arm braced against your leg, palm (and dumbbell) facing up. Bring your arm up, bending at the

279

280

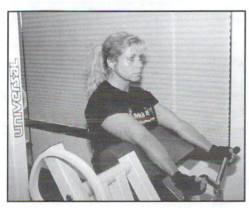

281

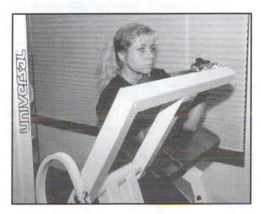

282

elbow. Your palm should face you as you complete the movement. Then, straighten your arm back out and repeat. (See figures 279–280.)

Using a machine, extend your arms straight out and grip the handle. Pull the handle toward you by bending your elbows. (Be sure your shoulders aren't doing the work.) Then extend your arms so that they are almost straight, and repeat. (See figures 281–282.)

Triceps extension

This exercise works the triceps muscle of the arm. It can be done using free weights or machine weights. To use free weights, hold a pair of dumbbells in your hands. Stand straight, with your elbow slightly bent. Move your arm straight back as if you were reaching behind you. Reach as far back as you can. Then move your arm back to the starting position. Repeat using the other arm. (See figures 283–284.) You can keep

283   284

285   286

your palm facing up or you can turn it to the side. The difference in hand position works two different parts of the triceps muscle.

To use machine weights, sit with your upper arms parallel to the ground. Grasp the handles. Then slowly straighten your arms, pulling the weight stack up. Move your arms back to the bent position and repeat. (See figure 285–286.)

Squat/leg press

This exercise works the thighs, calves and butt. Using free weights, it is called the squat; using machine weights it is called the leg press. If you're using free weights, you can use either dumbbells or a barbell. Because of a slightly higher level of difficulty, it should be performed with the aid of another person.

Using a pair of dumbbells, stand straight with your arms hanging down near your sides, a dumbbell in each hand. As always, keep your

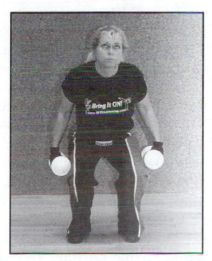

287

288

shoulders back, abs pulled in tight. Bend your knees as if you were about to sit in a chair. Squat as far as you can go, until your thighs are parallel to the floor. Slowly stand back up, pushing through the heels. (See figure 287.)

To do this exercise with a barbell, place the bar across your shoulders and hold it with both hands. Then, bend your knees as if you are about to sit in a chair, squatting until your thighs are parallel to the floor. Then return to a standing position. (See figure 288.)

If one is available, you may wish to use a Smith Machine. This machine is a barbell on a stand with hooks that "catch" the weight if you decide to stop or if the weight becomes unmanageable. This eliminates or reduces the need for a spotter.

289

290

291

figure 292

To build the quadriceps, keep your feet fairly close together (not quite shoulder-width apart). To work the hamstrings, glutes (butt), adductors and abductors (inner and outer thighs), stand with your feet wider than shoulder-width apart.

To use the leg press machine, lie on your back, knees bent at a 90 degree angle, calves parallel to the floor. Position your feet firmly on the foot plate. Make sure your shoulders fit snugly against the shoulder rest. Extend your legs forward, pushing the foot plate smoothly and evenly until your legs are straight. Then bend your knees until you are back in the starting position. (See figures 289–291.) As a variation, place only your toes on the plate and push. This exercises your calf muscles. (See figure 292.) As with the conventional and Smith Machine squats, if you widen your feet on the plate, it will work the hamstrings, glutes and thighs.

Hamstring curl

This exercise works the back of the thigh. It is usually done using a weight machine. Seat yourself so that your legs extend out in front of you and your calves rest on the padded bar. Then bend your knees until they reach about a 90 degree angle. Slowly extend your legs until they are straight. (See figures 293–294.)

293   294

Dead lift

This exercise builds stronger hamstrings and strengthens the lower back. It is usually performed with free weights. Stand holding dumbbells or a barbell in front of the body, legs less than a shoulder's width apart. Keep your shoulders back, your abs pulled in tight and your neck relaxed. Slowly inhale and, keeping your back straight, lower the weight as far as you can without losing your posture or stressing your back. Exhale, pushing through the heels and keeping your abs very tight, and raise the weights back up to starting position. Don't round your shoulders or back during this exercise. Perform it slowly and smoothly. If you feel strain in your back, decrease the weight and perform more repetitions. (See figures 295–297.)

  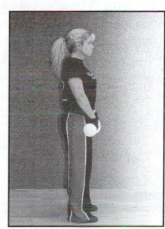

295   296   297

Leg Extension

This exercise works the front of the thigh (the quadriceps). It is usually done with a weight machine. Sit with your legs bent so that the top of your foot and the front of your shin cradle the padded bar. Then,

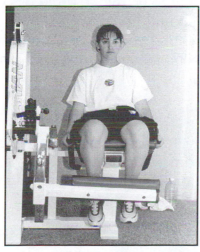 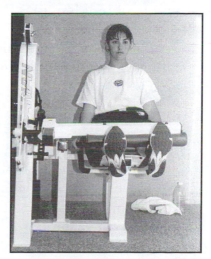

298   299

holding onto the handles that are located near your hips, straighten your legs and lift the bar. Then bend your knees to return to the starting position. (See figures 298–299.)

The advantages of strength training are many, but especially for women! The more muscle you build on your body, the less fat your body can store. Muscle tissue requires a lot of fuel to exist in its high metabolic state. You actually burn fat even while resting if you have a high ratio of lean muscle to fat on your body. Who wouldn't like to burn off fat while sleeping? Weight lifting also helps strengthen your bones, making women less susceptible to disabling osteoporosis in later life. Although muscle weighs much more than fat, it takes up almost four times less space on the body (think of body fat as "fluffy" and lean muscle as "dense.") So even though you may weigh the same or even more than you did before you began weight training, you may notice yourself wearing smaller sizes in clothing.

FOR WOMEN ONLY: The most important mathematical equation to remember is this one: speed times mass equals power. This means that even if you're small, you can still be powerful—you just have to be fast!

FOR WOMEN ONLY: Women are sometimes wary of weight lifting, thinking it will make them bulk up. This is not the case. Women don't bulk up the way men do, and can easily get defined rather than bulky muscles by lifting less weight for more repetitions. The ideal for muscle definition without bulking up is thought to be two to three sets of 10 to 12 repetitions each. This means you should lift enough weight so that the tenth repetition is very difficult to do. If you can easily do fifteen or more repetitions, the weight is too light and you're not doing your muscles much good.

DEBZ SAYS: If a person strength trains every day, she burns more muscle tissue for fuel to complete the work than she builds. This is why you see so many really gung-ho people at the gym every day who look like they never change much even though they work very hard all the time. It's BECAUSE they work so hard all the time! Alternate strength training with cardio training to maximize your body's fat burning capacity.

14
BEGINNER WORKOUT PLAN

The most important goal for a beginner is to learn to perform the techniques correctly. Therefore, your workouts should focus on these basics: learning and practicing the techniques, increasing conditioning and flexibility and building power. All of these fundamentals will serve you well as your kickboxing practice progresses.

Each workout session should consist of at least 5 to 10 minutes of warm-up and basic stretches, then the workout itself, then a cool down period with additional stretches. The training session itself does not have to be performed in the order shown below, although following a routine schedule can be helpful.

Warm up and stretches

5–10 minutes
Walk briskly, jump rope, jog slowly, slow shadow boxing
Neck stretch (page 17)
Shoulder stretches (page 18)
Shoulder shrug (page 19)
Back stretch (page 19)
Hip stretch (page 20)
Thigh stretch (page 20)
Hamstring stretch (page 21)
Knee stretch (page 22)
Ankle stretch (page 22)

Kicks

From neutral fighter's stance. Repeat each technique 10 times for each leg, then alternate legs. For each set of kicks, choose one target area and perform all kicks to that target area. For instance, perform the offensive front kick with your right leg forward. Kick 10 times to a low target, then switch your stance so that your left leg is forward. Kick 10 times to a low target. Switch your stance. Again perform an offensive front kick, kicking to the groin. (Although this is not legal in competition, it is good practice for self-defense). Switch legs. Then do the same to the abdomen. Switch legs and perform the defensive front kick, going through all the target areas. Practice each kick this way, then, if time permits, go through the entire routine again. Watch your technique in the mirror to make certain you're correctly performing the techniques. For the sake of convenience, knee strikes are included here (10 minutes).

Offensive front kick (practice kicking low, to groin and to abdomen) (page 28)

Defensive front kick (practice kicking low, to groin and to abdomen) (page 29).

Side kick (practice kicking low, to groin and to abdomen) (page 29, offensive; page 30, defensive)

Offensive roundhouse kick (practice kicking low, to groin, to abdomen and to head) (page 31)

Defensive roundhouse kick (practice kicking low, to groin, to abdomen and to head) (page 31)

Turn back kick (practice kicking to abdomen) (page 32)

Straight knee strike (page 34)

Side knee strike (page 34)

Punches

Practice the punches just as you practice the kicks. You may prefer to use a heavy bag as a target, or you can do the drill as shadow boxing, watching your techniques in the mirror. Elbow strikes are included here for convenience. These are not legal in competition but are useful in a self-defense situation. (10 minutes)

Jab (page 37)

Cross (page 38)

Hook (page 39)

Uppercut (page 39)

Overhand (page 40)

Spinning backfist (page 41)

Forward elbow strike (page 45)

Reverse elbow strike (page 45)

Upward elbow strike (page 45)

Side elbow strike (page 46)

Blocking and evading

Have a partner perform various techniques while you block. If you have no partner, perform the techniques as shadow boxing (5 minutes). As you gain confidence in your technique, begin using speed bags, double end bags, and similar training devices for those times when you're working out solo.

Catching (page 49)
Cupping (page 49)
Hooking (page 49)
Parrying (page 50)
Shin block (page 51)
Knee-elbow block (page 52)
Double arm block (page 52)
Reinforced double arm block (page 52)
Clinch (page 53)
Thai thigh block (page 53)
Forearm-elbow block (page 53)
Ducking (page 54)
Slipping (page 54)
Duck and slip combination (page 55)

Conditioning, speed and strength drills

Not all drills need to be done each session. Pick and choose depending on availability of partners and areas needing improvement (15–20 minutes).

Clench-and-release exercise (page 95)
Punching drill (page 96)
Frog jumps (page 98)
Jumping drill (page 98)
Crunches (with variations) (page 99)
Boxer situps (page 100)
Push-ups (with variations) (page 101)
Pull-ups (page 102)
Flutter kicks, scissors kicks or leg lifts (page 104)
Rope ups (page 105)
Slow motion kicking (page 105)

Weight lifting

Do not do this every day (20–30 minutes).
Chest press/bench press (page 109)
Butterfly press/bench fly (page 111)
Lateral pull down (page 112)
Lateral raise (page 112)

Biceps curl (page 113)
Triceps extension (page 115)
Squat/leg press (page 116)
Hamstring curl (page 117)
Dead lift (page 118)
Leg extension (page 119)

Cool down

Perform with flexibility exercises (5 - 10 minutes).
Side bend (page 91)
Hip rotation (page 91)
Calf stretch (page 92)
Body bridge (page 92)
Groin lift (page 93)
Hamstring lift (page 93)

FOR WOMEN ONLY: Don't beat yourself up if you have a bad day, miss training because you're ill or gobbled down half a New York-style cheese-cake because your boyfriend decided he doesn't feel comfortable dating a strong, determined woman! Accept your slip-ups as human nature, then re-focus as soon as possible.

DEBZ SAYS: Be sure you're drinking plenty of water! Don't use thirst as an indicator of when it's time to take in more fluid. An athlete training this hard should be drinking a minimum of 2 ounces of water per pound of body weight per day to avoid dehydration. 3 ounces per pound of body weight is best. Carry a water bottle with you at all times and fill it when it's empty. Remember, the body is made up primarily of water. To function at your peak, mentally and physically, you must keep hydrated!

15
INTERMEDIATE WORKOUT PLAN

At the intermediate level, one must continue mastering the techniques, but is ready to begin combining them into series and is ready to begin practice sparring. Conditioning and strength exercises, as well as flexibility exercises, are still important.

Each workout session should include warm-ups and stretches, the workout itself, and a cool down period with stretches.

Warm-up and stretches

(5–10 minutes)
Walk briskly, jump rope, jog slowly, slow shadow boxing
Neck stretch (page 17)
Shoulder stretches (page 18)
Shoulder shrug (page 19)
Back stretch (page 19)
Hip stretch (page 20)
Thigh stretch (page 20)
Hamstring stretch (page 21)
Knee stretch (page 22)
Ankle stretch (page 22)

Kicks

From neutral fighter's stance. Repeat each technique 10 times for each leg, then alternate legs. For each set of kicks, choose one target area and perform all kicks to that target area, just as you did for the beginner plan. Watch your technique in the mirror to make certain you're correctly performing the techniques. For the sake of convenience, knee strikes are included here (5 minutes).

Offensive front kick (practice kicking low, to groin and to abdomen) (page 28)

Defensive front kick (practice kicking low, to groin and to abdomen) (page 29)

Side kick (practice kicking low, to groin and to abdomen) (page 29, offense; page 30, defense)

Offensive roundhouse kick (practice kicking low, to groin, to abdomen and to head) (page 31)

Defensive roundhouse kick (practice kicking low, to groin, to abdomen and to head) (page 32)

Turn back kick (practice kicking to abdomen) (page 32)

Straight knee strike (page 34)

Side knee strike (page 34)

Punches

Practice the punches just as you practice the kicks. You may prefer to use a heavy bag as a target, or you can do the drill as shadow boxing, watching your techniques in the mirror. Elbow strikes are included here for convenience. These are not legal in competition but are useful in a self-defense situation (5 minutes).

Jab (page 37)

Cross (page 38)

Hook (page 39)

Uppercut (page 39)

Overhand (page 40)

Spinning backfist (page 41)

Forward elbow strike (page 45)

Reverse elbow strike (page 45)

Upward elbow strike (page 45)

Side elbow strike (page 46)

Kicking Combinations

(5 minutes)

Front kick-roundhouse kick combination (page 68)

Side kick-turn kick combination (page 70)

Roundhouse kick-side kick Combination (page 72)

Low roundhouse kick-high roundhouse kick combination (page 74)

Numbers game (page 76)

Chase game (page 77)

Hi-lo game (page 77)

Punching combinations

(5 minutes)
Jab-cross combination (page 80)
Jab-cross-hook combination (page 81)
Jab-uppercut (page 81)
Jab-spinning backfist (page 81)
Jab-overhand (page 81)

Punch-kick combinations

(5 minutes)
Jab-roundhouse combination (page 85)
Jab-cross-rear knee strike (page 85)
Front kick-jab-cross (page 86)
Side kick-jab-cross (page 87)
Roundhouse kick-jab-cross-roundhouse kick combination (page 87)

Blocking and evading

Have a partner perform various techniques while you block. If you
have no partner, perform the techniques as shadow boxing (5 minutes).
Catching (page 49)
Cupping (page 49)
Hooking (page 49)
Parrying (page 50)
Shin block (page 51)
Knee-elbow block (page 52)
Double arm block (page 52)
Reinforced double arm block (page 52)
Clinch (page 53)
Thai thigh block (page 53)
Forearm-elbow block (page 53)
Ducking (page 54)
Slipping (page 54)
Duck and slip combination (page 55)

Footwork

Have a partner strike at you with various techniques. Use footwork
to avoid being struck. Shadow box if a partner is unavailable (5 min-
utes).
Forward stepping (page 56)
Backward stepping (page 58)
Side stepping (page 59)

Pivot stepping (page 60)

Shadow boxing

Putting it all together. Try punching, kicking, blocking, evading and footwork (3-minute rounds, 6 minutes).

Practice sparring

Putting it all together—with a partner. Decide on how much contact you're comfortable with (no contact, light contact, heavy contact). Put on your equipment and get ready to fight! (3-minute rounds). Be sure to ask your partner for a constructive critique after each round and practice improving weak areas, (6–9 minutes).

Conditioning, speed and strength drills

Not all drills need to be done each session. Pick and choose depending on availability of partners and areas needing improvement (15–20 minutes).

Clench-and-release Exercise (page 95)
Punching drill (page 96)
Slipping drill (page 96)
Hand reaction time drill (page 96)
Foot reaction time drill: (page 97)
Foot reaction drill (page 97)
Frog jumps (page 98)
Jumping drill (page 98)
Crunches (with variations) (page 99)
Boxer sit-ups (page 100)
Push-ups (with variations) (page 101)
Pull-ups (page 102)
Leg lifts (page 104)
Rope ups (page 105)
Slow motion kicking (page 105)

Weight lifting

Do not do this every day (20 - 30 minutes).
Chest press/bench press (page 109)
Butterfly press/bench fly (page 111)
Lateral pull down (page 112)
Lateral raise (page 112)
Biceps curl (page 113)
Triceps extension (page 115)

Squat/leg press (page 116)
Hamstring curl (page 117)
Dead lift (page 118)
Leg extension (page 119)

Cool down with flexibility exercises

(5–10 minutes)
Side bend (page 91)
Hip rotation (page 91)
Calf stretch (page 92)
Body bridge (page 92)
Groin lift (page 93)
Hamstring lift (page 93)

FOR WOMEN ONLY: As you gain more experience kickboxing, you may find yourself changing in ways you didn't anticipate. Some women report that they became more assertive after they started training. Others discovered fears they never realized they had. This is a natural part of combat training, especially for women. Accept it, and realize that the emotional hurdles, while bumpy, will lead to worthwhile personal growth in the long run.

DEBZ SAYS: Keep your goals in full view every day and review how you plan to achieve them. This will help you get through any crisis. Also, it's good to note: Goals change sometimes. Your original goal may have been to get into shape and it might end up with you becoming certified to teach others! As long as you make positive moves forward in life, you are successful!

16
ADVANCED WORKOUT PLAN

As an advanced kickboxer, you will continue to work on perfecting techniques, but will spend more time sparring with partners. You may also add aerobic workouts, such as jogging, in addition to your kickboxing workouts. You're ready to develop your own combinations and to try them out.

You'll still need to plan for warm-ups and stretches and for cooling down with stretches.

Warm-up and stretches

(5–10 minutes)
Walk briskly, jump rope, jog slowly, slow shadow boxing
Neck stretch (page 17)
Shoulder stretches (page 18)
Shoulder shrug (page 19)
Back stretch (page 19)
Hip stretch (page 20)
Thigh stretch (page 20)
Hamstring stretch (page 21)
Knee stretch (page 22)
Ankle stretch (page 22)

Kicks

From neutral fighter's stance. Repeat each technique 10 times for each leg, then alternate legs just as you did for the beginner and intermediate levels. Watch your technique in the mirror to make certain you're correctly performing the techniques. For the sake of convenience, knee strikes are included here (5 minutes).

Offensive front kick (practice kicking low, to groin and to abdomen) (page 25)

Defensive front kick (practice kicking low, to groin and to abdomen) (page 24)

Side kick (practice kicking low, to groin and to abdomen) (page 29, offense; 30, defense)

Offensive roundhouse kick (practice kicking low, to groin, to abdomen and to head) (page 31)

Defensive roundhouse kick (practice kicking low, to groin, to abdomen and to head) (page 31)

Turn back kick (practice kicking to abdomen) (page 32)

Straight knee strike (page 34)

Side knee strike (page 34)

Punches

Practice the punches just as you practice the kicks. You may prefer to use a heavy bag as a target, or you can do the drill as shadow boxing, watching your techniques in the mirror. Elbow strikes are included here for convenience. These are not legal in competition but are useful in a self-defense situation (5 minutes).

Jab (page 37)

Cross (page 38)

Hook (page 39)

Uppercut (page 39)

Overhand (page 40)

Spinning backfist (page 41)

Forward elbow strike (page 45)

Reverse elbow strike (page 45)

Upward elbow strike (page 45)

Side elbow strike (page 46)

Kicking combinations

You decide which combinations work for you (5 minutes).

Numbers game (page 76)

Chase game (page 77)

Hi-lo game (page 77)

Punching combinations

You decide which combinations work for you (5 minutes).

Punch-kick combinations

You decide which combinations work for you (5 minutes).

Blocking and Evading

Have a partner perform various techniques while you block. If you have no partner, perform the techniques as shadow boxing (5 minutes).

Catching (page 49)
Cupping (page 49)
Hooking (page 49)
Parrying (page 50)
Shin block (page 51)
Knee-elbow block (page 52)
Double arm block (page 52)
Reinforced double arm block (page 52)
Clinch (page 53)
Thai thigh block (page 53)
Forearm-elbow block (page 53)
Ducking (page 54)
Slipping (page 54)
Duck and slip combination (page 55)

Footwork

Have a partner strike at you with various techniques. Use footwork to avoid being struck. Shadow box if a partner is unavailable (5 minutes).

Forward stepping (page 56)
Backward stepping (page 58)
Side stepping (page 59)
Pivot stepping (page 60)

Shadow boxing

Putting it all together. Try punching, kicking, blocking, evading and footwork (3-minute rounds, 9–12 minutes).

Practice sparring

Putting it all together—with a partner. Decide on how much contact you're comfortable with (no contact, light contact, heavy contact). Put on your equipment and get ready to fight! (3-minute rounds, 12–15 minutes).

Conditioning, speed and strength drills

Not all drills need to be done each session. Pick and choose depending on availability of partners and areas needing improvement (15–20 minutes).

Clench-and-release exercise (page 95)
Punching drill (page 96)
Slipping drill (page 96)
Hand reaction time drill (page 96)
Foot reaction time drill: (page 97)
Foot reaction drill (page 97)
Frog jumps (page 98)
Jumping drill (page 98)
Crunches (with variations) (page 99)
Boxer sit-ups (page 100)
Push-ups (with variations) (page 101)
Pull-ups (page 102)
Leg lifts (page 104)
Rope ups (page 105)
Slow motion kicking (page 105)

Weight lifting

Do not do this every day (20–30 minutes).
Chest press/bench press (page 109)
Butterfly press/bench fly (page 111)
Lateral pull down (page 112)
Lateral raise (page 112)
Biceps curl (page 113)
Triceps extension (page 115)
Squat/leg press (page 116)
Hamstring curl (page 117)
Dead lift (page 118)
Leg extension (page 119)

Cool down with flexibility exercises

(5–10 minutes).
Side bend (page 91)
Hip rotation (page 91)
Calf stretch (page 92)
Body bridge (page 92)
Groin lift (page 93)
Hamstring lift (page 93)

FOR WOMEN ONLY: At the advanced level, you're working harder and more efficiently than ever before. You've joined the ranks of elite athletes ... and maybe it's taking a toll on your body. Your nutritional needs are very different now than they were when you first started training. You may need many more calories than you did previously, and perhaps your eating habits are not as good as they could be. Take the time to meet with a dietician or nutritionist who has worked with superior athletes to create a dietary plan that suits your needs.

DEBZ SAYS: Your preconceived ideas of what's feminine and appropriate for women to do may be holding you back from achieving all you can in your kickboxing career. Now's the time to re-examine some of your old attitudes and toss them out if they don't match up with the person you're trying to be!

17
AMATEUR AND PRO BOUTS

If you're interested in "real" competition—competing in amateur or pro bouts with people you don't spar every day in class, there are some things you need to know.

Amateur competition starts at age 10, although the wisdom of allowing your fifth grader in the ring could be debated. You can continue competing no matter how old you are, although at certain ages you may need to get a physical examination before you enter the ring. (The sanctioning organization or tournament organizer will tell you this information.) If you want to test your skills, or if you're thinking about turning pro, amateur bouts are the place to start.

To find an amateur competition, ask your coach or at your gym. If neither can help you, join one of the recognized sanctioning organizations and get on the mailing list. Some good organizations are the World Kickboxing Association, World Kickboxing Council, International Kickboxing Federation, the United States Amateur Kickboxing Association and the International Sport Kickboxing Association.

It's always best to start with a competition close to home before spending time and energy on international flights (and fights) although at some time you may want to see how you stack up to the foreign competition.

These sanctioning organizations rank amateurs (who don't, of course, make money from their fights) according to their success in the ring. You can compete for titles. Once you're an established amateur, it's easier to turn pro and get paying matches.

Amateurs must wear safety equipment, including headgear, mouthguard, shin pads and gloves. Amateurs often meet in tournaments that allow many different kickboxers at many different skill levels to compete. To prepare for such competition, you will need to ramp up your training. Like any other athlete, you need to prepare for such matches several weeks ahead of time so that you're in top shape with razor-sharp reflexes when you step into the ring. See Chapter 19 for further informa-

135

tion on training for amateur and pro bouts. You will also need to make sure you understand the tournament/competition rules and that the competition is sponsored by a reputable person or organization.

Fighters are matched according to the weight classes listed here:

Less than 117 lbs: Atomweight
117 - 119.9: Flyweight
120 - 124.9: Bantamweight
125 - 132.9: Featherweight
133 - 137.9: Lightweight
138 - 142.9: Super lightweight
143 - 147.9: Welterweight
148 - 154.9: Light middleweight
155 - 160.9: Middleweight
161 - 168.9: Super middleweight
169 - 179.9: Light heavyweight
180 - 189.9: Cruiserweight
190 - 209.9: Heavyweight
Over 210: Super heavyweight

Scoring

Amateurs usually fight three rounds of two minutes, with a one minute rest between. Rarely, rounds will go three minutes (usually only Thai kickboxing does this). Kids fight one minute rounds. For championship title matches, each round lasts three minutes.

Each round is scored on a 10 point system. The winner of each round—the one who delivers the most effective punches and kicks—wins 10 points. At the end of the match, the points are totaled and someone wins. However, you lose points if you're knocked down but get up again. If you don't get up again, you don't just lose points, you lose the match. You also lose points if you're disoriented by a stunning blow. Each of these minor disasters will cost you a point. The referee gives a standing eight count if you appear disoriented. If you can shake it off by the time he or she reaches 8, you're allowed to continue. Usually the referee will end the match if you're knocked down three times.

Full contact kickboxing

This used to be known as full contact karate. The rules are slightly different than for amateur kickboxing. Equipment, including mouthguard, shin guards and gloves, is required. Headgear is not required. Matches are between four and 12 rounds, depending on the sanctioning organizations, with championship title fights going 12 rounds and others going fewer. All kicks must hit above the waist. Kicks to the legs and knee strikes are illegal. Both fighters must perform a minimum of eight kicks per round. Otherwise, the fighter is penalized one point.

International kickboxing

International kickboxing is more lucrative than full contact kickboxing, and it has slightly different rules. Depending on where you fight, matches go between five and 12 rounds. Rounds last two or three minutes each, depending on the sponsoring organization. You can kick anywhere to the body except the groin. In some competitions, knee strikes are allowed. There is no minimum number of kicks. Only boxing gloves and mouthguards are required. Other equipment is optional.

Muay Thai kickboxing

This is only for the hardcore kickboxer. Thai kickboxers wear gloves and that's about it. (Groin protectors for the men are required.) Mouthguards are optional. Rounds last three minutes and there are five rounds per match with two minute rests between each round. Knee and elbow strikes are allowed. Any target area is legal except the groin.

Pro fighting

To become a pro fighter, you need a manager. A manager helps guide your career. He or she sets up your fights and makes sure you get paid. For this, your manager gets a cut of your earnings, usually between 10 and 30 percent. Your manager should care about you as much (or more) than money. He or she should have a plan for your career and should have good connections in order to get you good fights, publicity and maybe even an endorsement deal. There are plenty of disreputable managers around, so choose carefully.

To fight pro, you need a license in most states. These are usually issued by the state athletic commission or the state labor board. You have to pass a physical examination and may be tested for AIDS, HIV, hepatitis and other blood-borne diseases. If you don't follow the rules, your license will be yanked. The state can even withhold part of your fight purse—your earnings from a fight—if you misbehave. Promoters must also be licensed; this is supposed to ensure safe fights. Fight promoters put together fights, finding a place to hold matches, getting the word out, and coming up with the prize purse. Referees are also licensed by the state and are assigned to fights by the state commission.

The K-1 Grand Prix tournament is the most prestigious kickboxing competition in the world, with the winner earning $300,000. But women aren't allowed to compete, although they may get their chance in the near future. Even for men, there is very little money in pro kickboxing, so you should realize that you're not going to retire wealthy. You will need to have a day job, preferably one with flexibility so you can train. And remember, as kickboxing grows in popularity, so will your opportunities.

Turning pro: a kickboxer reflects on choices

Penny DeGraw, a kickboxer, talks about her feelings on turning pro:

I have been training to fight for two weeks now. My new trainer, Philip, is the greatest guy. I have progressed dramatically under his care. He makes me run, something I don't care to do, but he runs with me so I have conversation (as long as I can breathe) and companionship. Luckily the farthest we have to run is just under two miles, which is far enough in the Georgia heat and humidity.

After running we either do technique drills or stamina drills and then we spar. I can already tell that my reaction time is quicker and my combinations are getting easier, in the way that I don't have to think about individual punches or kick as much as I'm just making an attack to spaces which I think are open.

What about this fight? I have yet to step into a ring against an unknown opponent. I have yet to fight someone who is a woman, approximately my size, and of similar ability. I wonder what that will be like. I get boosts of confidence by sparring someone less trained than me (mostly the women) and then get frustrated when I spar with the men who are bigger, faster and have years of experience. I can't be sure how I should measure up to them and when I get punched in the nose, get angry at myself for not keeping a basic guard up in front of my face.

The crowd aspect of a match is something I don't think will bother me at all. I have been in front of crowds before and as long as I'm not expected to speak (or sing), I don't mind. In fact, I've always been somewhat of a showboat, a "look at me" sort of person. My little brother is like that, too, and having to compete against him for attention has kept the drive strong, even now. I'm already getting good attention. So many people at the gym have stopped to say "hi" to me and they all seem to know that I'm training for a "real" fight. Everyone wants to come see it and they keep asking me when and where.

I must admit that I also like that we do the most training in the late afternoons and early evenings when there are the most people in the gym. Then when it's just Philip and me in the ring, we draw watchers from the classes. I know that part of it is to get attention to Philip as a trainer so he can draw future clients from the exposure, but even that fact that he's "using" my training to this end is flattering. I want to be a good fighter so he is considered a good trainer as much as I just want to be a winner for myself. It is a very important relationship that you have, you and your trainer. It takes more trust than other coaching situations that I've been familiar with like gymnastics or team sports. In this case, al-

most everything I know I get from my coach, and if he doesn't give me everything I need, the consequences can be more serious than just a loss of a match.

That makes me think of why I'm doing this. I got into it almost accidentally. A friend who does jujitsu asked me to stop in and give it a try and since I'm an aging ex-gymnast, I've been needing some kind of physical activity that can help keep my whole body in shape similar to the way it once was when I was younger and more flexible. I did the aerobic kickboxing for about six months before I ever learned any defense and stepped into the ring to spar. I was a mess that first time. I had no idea what to expect and when this other girl started to come at me, throwing punches, I didn't know what to do. Oddly enough, I did react and fought back well enough that onlookers didn't know what was happening inside, until the bell sounded, and I retreated to the corner and was reduced to tears from the exhaustion of anxiety and physical exertion.

The best thing at that point was that the coach reassured me that I did just fine and that I looked good doing it. The next couple of days were spent on introspection. I remember that I was very shaken in my security. I always assumed that if I got into some kind of situation, I could handle myself. But there I was, facing a girl not much bigger than me, and much younger than me, and I couldn't handle it. I started looking at strangers differently. There were so many people out in this world that could do me harm if they tried, and I was afraid.

After a couple more days, I saw that the world hadn't changed overnight and that I needn't be afraid of everyone but that I needed more confidence in my own abilities. I returned to the defense classes and went back into the ring to face my fear and see if I couldn't overcome it.

I can't say that I have completely overcome that fear yet, and I hope I never really do. There's a good feeling of anxiety and a rush of adrenaline when you put on headgear and slip in a mouthpiece that appeals to my adventurous side. Now I want to see if I can not only fend off an opponent but get in a few good shots as well. Now it's a serious game that I have learned to play and want to play well.

I'm beginning to dream about fighting. As I'm drifting off to sleep, I usually find myself sparring with someone and wake myself up as I throw up an arm to block a punch or jerk a leg to throw a kick at my opponent. That is an interesting phenomena. Then I have had dreams about the match day itself. One was where I was told that I didn't have an opponent and wasn't going to fight and then a little later they came and said, "What are you doing? You're up next." Then I couldn't find my trainer and started panicking. That wasn't really much of a dream, more a nightmare. I woke up before it went much further, but who knows what each night's sleep will bring.

FOR WOMEN ONLY: Women sometimes get criticized for turning pro. Some people claim pro female fighters are "exploited." If you turn pro, be ready for questions men would never be asked, such as, "What does your mother/husband/child think?" or "Aren't you afraid of losing your looks?" Practice answering politely and be thankful for the publicity!

FOR WOMEN ONLY: Not a lot of women fight on the pro circuit. It makes sense to find out what weight the competition fights at. In order to have competition, you may need to bulk up or slim down to a more popular weight.

DEBZ SAYS: Pro fighters don't make a lot of money—especially women. So you'll need a day job. Why not train other kickboxers? This will give you the flexibility you need to follow a pro training schedule, plus you'll be passing on your knowledge. The world needs more women teaching combat sports! You can get certified as a personal trainer after a short period of intensive study and testing, and you can help others get into and stay in shape. You can set your own hours, and in some areas of the country, the money is very good!

18
DEVELOPING FIGHTING SKILLS

Many women find the thought of fighting appealing but the actual practice of it can be very difficult for them. They might be afraid of getting hurt or of hurting other people. If you're hesitant about this aspect of kickboxing, there are several approaches you can take. First, you can enroll in an aerobic kickboxing class that won't require physical contact with partners. As you become more confident, you may wish to begin training in a regular kickboxing class. A second step might be to enroll in an aerobic kickbox class that incorporates bag work in order to become more accustomed to contact.

Or, if you want to train in kickboxing but need some extra time to prepare for sparring, talk it over with your coach. One of the best ways to introduce women to the realities of sparring is through step sparring, which is sparring under carefully controlled conditions, and no-contact sparring, in which partners attack and defend as in a regular sparring match but at enough distance so they do not actually make contact. From here, women can move to light contact matches where each partner rigidly controls how powerful her kicks and punches are.

Step sparring, a method of practicing fighting techniques in combinations, helps prepare you for freestyle sparring or possible confrontations. Learning to hit others and being hit yourself can be difficult for women, since few of us have much experience with contact sports, especially as adults. By following a series of carefully controlled and planned techniques, you can learn to master fighting techniques and will soon feel confident about your ability to withstand an attack.

Step sparring, which might also be called controlled sparring, helps you learn without feeling overwhelmed or pressured by an actual sparring match. For this reason, beginning kickboxers may find step sparring most useful, although even advanced fighters may want to use step sparring on occasion, particularly when incorporating new techniques into their sparring.

Step sparring allows you to try out techniques not allowed in regular sparring matches. At its basic level, step sparring is done like this: one partner attacks the other with one technique—a kick or a punch. The defending partner blocks the kick or punch, using the appropriate technique. As the defending partner grows more confident, she will use more sophisticated techniques, such as footwork or slipping to avoid the strike and will actually counter-attack with a technique of her own. As each partner grows more confident, the step sparring moves faster (closer to the tempo of a regular sparring match). Keep in mind that in step sparring, you're allowed to use techniques, such as elbow strikes and strikes to the groin, that you cannot use in regular sparring. This makes it a useful practice for self-defense scenarios.

Although step sparring requires a partner to be most effective, you can practice shadow step sparring by yourself. You can also use a heavy bag as an opponent, if you want to practice your techniques full speed, at full force. Simply imagine that an opponent is kicking or punching, and respond. For this purpose, a hanging heavy bag is more realistic than a freestanding heavy bag, since it moves back and forth as you kick and punch.

Use care when working with partners. Never use full force against a partner. Limit contact to light touch, especially at first. Once you're more confident in your skills, you may wish to practice with heavier contact, but be certain your partner agrees, and always listen if he or she asks you to lighten up. Wear sparring equipment whenever you spar, even with light or no contact; this can help prevent accidents from turning into injuries.

Sparring matches

Although step sparring helps you learn new techniques, counters and defensive maneuvers, you must actually fight in sparring matches to become a proficient kickboxer.

In a regular sparring match, you perform different techniques against an opponent, with the intention of scoring a point, while your opponent is trying to score a point against you. Partners move back and forth within the ring exchanging techniques and trying to block, avoid and counter one another's movements.

Such sparring is not intended to mimic a street fight or confrontation. Instead, it is a means for you to practice your techniques, to learn about timing and to face opponents of both genders, various sizes and many skill levels. Although you never know what might happen in a street fight, sparring practice can help you prepare for such a possibility. Just keep in mind that an attacker in a street fight isn't going to follow the "rules"—he or she will grab your hair, kick you in the groin, and use elbow strikes and other illegal techniques. He or she might also have a weapon. Thus, it's important not to become too overconfident of your self-defense skills, and to realize that the best self-defense is being able to walk away from a confrontation before it turns into a fight.

Getting hit

For most women, the hardest part of sparring isn't using difficult techniques or scoring points or defending against kicks to the head. The hardest part of sparring is getting hit. Less difficult, but still challenging, is actually hitting other people. Men often participate in contact sports throughout their lives, but women don't tend to. We're not accustomed to getting hit and can find the process intimidating. Most of us were taught from birth to nurture others and to avoid conflict. It goes against everything we know to physically confront another person.

First, realize that becoming comfortable with physical contact is simply a matter of practice. Men tend to be more physical beings than women; they punch their buddies, roughhouse with their kids, play basketball hard. If they don't come home with bruises, they're disappointed. Women hug their friends, kiss their kids, and work out on treadmills. Of course getting kicked in the head is disorienting the first time or two.

Second, practice with sensitive partners—people who are willing to slow down, to use very light contact (if any), and to listen to you and offer encouragement.

Third, and finally, practice your techniques so that you're hitting *something*, whether it's a heavy bag or a target you rig up yourself. Getting accustomed to contact requires practice and you should obtain that practice any way you can.

Sparring basics

Beginning fighters often spar very far away from each other in order to avoid contact (which can be a little scary) and because they don't have confidence in their control. When they realize the problem, they sometimes go to the opposite extreme, sparring so close to each other that no techniques can be used effectively. Learn fighting range by step sparring and put this knowledge to use in sparring. Go slowly, but try to make light contact with your partner in order to build your confidence.

To begin a sparring match, agree to a time limit and a ring size. Assume a fighter's stance. When you're ready, wait for the signal. The coach will give it. Then simply begin fighting.

To stop the match at any time, so that you can fix a piece of equipment or because you sprained your ankle, hold up your hands, yell "time" or "stop," and step away from your partner. Don't turn your back. If your partner hasn't heard you, you could get hurt. In an official match, stepping out like this is an automatic forfeit, but there is no need to be so formal in practice sparring. In an official match, if your equipment comes loose or you're injured, the referee will stop the match and allow you the opportunity to fix your equipment or assess your injury. This will not automatically disqualify you.

Watch your partner's eyes at all times as you spar. This gives you clues as to what he or she plans to do next. Besides, if you're watching her left leg, you won't see the right punch coming. Keep your eyes up and your mind focused on the match at all times.

During practice sparring, it is courteous to acknowledge any points your partner scores. This can be done by nodding your head, saying "point," or tapping the target area where the point scored. This informal system allows partners to assess how they're doing and learn what techniques are effective. However, you will find that some partners won't do this because they don't want to give any psychological advantage to their "opponent." That's okay, too. You may find that you prefer sparring this way. But remember that practice sparring sessions are intended to make you a better fighter, and if you never have the opportunity to learn how you're doing, such matches are almost useless. Make sure you take the time to talk with your partner after a sparring session to learn what worked and what didn't, and be sure your coach helps you incorporate what you've learned in your sparring.

Timing techniques

The best way to improve your sparring performance is simply to practice sparring. However, some drills, called timing techniques, can enhance your skills, quicken your reflexes and improve your sparring. Timing techniques help you to see openings in your partner's guard and to strike immediately. Not only do these drills help you see the openings, they help you *anticipate* the openings, to know that they're coming and that you'll be ready.

Understanding timing techniques

To understand timing techniques, you have to understand that each fighting technique has inherent strengths and weaknesses. As a fighter, you hope to exploit the technique's weakness when you're defending, and to use its strengths when you're attacking.

For example, the roundhouse kick is an excellent technique for scoring high. Even people with limited flexibility can kick head high with a roundhouse kick. It can also be very fast, and therefore hard to block or avoid. Its weakness, however, is that you can leave your chest open and unguarded when you perform it. A good opponent will spot this and immediately strike to your chest.

If you've been practicing timing techniques, you know this weakness. Therefore, if your partner uses a roundhouse kick, you'll move immediately to exploit its weakness. And, since you understand this weakness, you'll attempt to compensate for it when you use the technique yourself. For instance, you can practice the technique keeping both arms and hands up to protect your chest and head.

Ideally, you should work with a partner to hone your skills, but you can practice timing techniques on a heavy bag or in front of a mirror.

Practice the following drills, then devise your own depending on the techniques you use. All of the drills listed below follow a similar sequence, that you can vary as you grow more comfortable with the drills.

Blocking and countering drills

Beginning fighters should block the opponent's techniques to avoid the attack and to prevent the opponent from scoring. Then launch your own attack, which is called the counter or counter-attack. In the beginning stages, keep these counter-attacks simple. Use more sophisticated counters as you grow more skilled.

Blocking and countering punches and kicks

Partners assume fighter's stances. The attacking partner punches or kicks to your midsection with her forward hand. Block this strike with any of the blocks you've learned. Practice until you're comfortable deflecting your partner's hand or foot away. Then add a countering technique of your own, such as a jab or a roundhouse kick. You need to time this technique so that you launch your attack just as you're deflecting the block; this leaves your partner open for your strike. Add more techniques if your partner remains open. (See figures 300 - 304 on the following page).

Countering strikes without blocking

As you grow more skilled and practice your timing techniques, you'll no longer block an attack before countering. Blocking takes time and commits you to a technique that cannot score a point. In sparring, where every second counts, this is a drawback. (Of course, in every sparring match, you'll have

300

301

302

303

304

to block attacks, but the more often you can avoid it, the better your sparring will be.) Instead of blocking, use footwork and evasion (ducking and slipping) to avoid a technique and then counter with one of your own attacks. The following techniques will get you started.

Evading and countering a punch

Partners should assume fighter's stances. The attacking partner performs a jab. Step to the side (away from the punch) and strike to the opponent's midsection or ribcage with any technique. (You can also use angle stepping to avoid the punch and get into range.) (See figures 305–307.)

305

306

307

308

309

310

Evading and countering a kick

Partners assume fighter's stances. The attacking partner performs a kick with her forward leg. Instead of blocking the kick, step away from the strike (moving toward your partner's body) and strike with a technique of your own to the middle section. (See figures 308–310.)

Countering with kicks

Basic timing techniques require you put to use much of what you've learned about footwork and speed. You learn to determine the type of technique your partner is using before it strikes. As your skill grows, you can block or counter these techniques more consistently. As you gain skill, you learn to counter your partner's techniques using kicks without blocking. Unlike avoiding a strike and then stepping forward and punching, countering with a kick still leaves you in kicking range, where you're less vulnerable. Using a kick to counter a strike is faster as well. You can perform your kick—your counterattack—even before your partner has finished striking.

Countering with turn back kicks

Both partners assume fighter's stances. The attacking partner performs a sidekick using her front leg. As soon as she chambers her leg for the kick, immediately turn and perform a turn back kick to your partner's midsection. Don't try to block the kick first and then perform your own kick. By turning to do the turn back kick, you'll avoid your partner's kick and can take advantage of the opening that will follow. You can also add a backfist after the reverse kick to increase your chances of scoring. (See figures 311–314.) This technique also works against turn back kicks and roundhouse kicks.

You can develop other timing techniques based on your particular strengths. Using timing techniques can help you learn to spot openings and take advantage of them. They can help you become a more confident, aggressive fighter, which benefits you in the ring.

Sparring bigger people

Women should always spar male partners when they have the chance, since in a confrontation, you're more likely to have to defend yourself against a man. In addition, men are generally taller and heavier than women, and so

311   312

313   *314*

you have to fight them differently. It is extremely important to understand how to modify your techniques and sparring habits to suit the opponent you face. While it is true that when fighting in sanctioned amateur or professional bouts, you'll fight only those people who weigh about the same as you do, many of your practice sparring matches will be against partners who are taller and heavier. Also, consider that even when fighting someone in the same weight class, that person might be taller and have a longer reach, or might be smaller but more muscular (and therefore more powerful).

Don't let someone else's size intimidate you. Stay focused. Think only of sparring to the best of your ability. Motivation may be key here: would you fight better or smarter if you were having to defend your child? If you were experiencing an attempted rape? Finally getting one over on your neanderthal boss?

In order to get the most from your sparring efforts, take an honest inventory of your body type. Are you shorter than most of the people you spar? Are you heavier or lighter than most other women? How do you compare to your male sparring partners? Keep in mind that speed counters mass, so even if you're smaller than your opponent, you can be faster, and therefore just as powerful. If you're lighter in weight and have less muscle mass, you can be more flexible, which means that your roundhouse kick can be higher and faster.

For many women, fighting in close (within punching range) works well. It neutralizes the bigger person's height advantage. In-close fighting can be used successfully against people who like to counter defensively. If you're in punching range, it's more difficult for them to counter your techniques.

You can use kicks to manuever into and out of punching range. One way to do this is to feint with a kick, much as you jab with your fist, to feel the opponent out. Then, instead of returning your foot to its original position, drop it right in front of your opponent. Now you're in punching range, so you can slide or step in with a punch. You can also use a kick to push yourself out of range. Don't forget footwork; staying light on your feet is essential. The key here is moving in and out as quickly as possible. This keeps you in control of the match and helps you capitalize on your strengths and minimize your weaknesses.

Many female kickboxers find themselves frustrated when they kick their sparring opponent and essentially bounce off him. The best way to prevent this recoiling of energy (which is a problem not limited to women, but since we're smaller, it does happen to us more) is through practice.

When you kick full power against a heavy, inflexible target, especially with a technique that's new to you, your body can't account for the sudden energy of the strike, so the energy recoils back on you and you bounce off your target. This only happens when your target doesn't absorb some of the energy, such as by stepping back. To solve this problem, practice doing full contact techniques. Learn to control the kick, redistribute your weight, and maintain your balance while focusing your energy on striking to and through the target. If you do the technique correctly, the target (your opponent) will absorb most, if not all, of your energy. Heavy bag training is a necessity for this. A heavy bag is like a person; you can kick it pretty hard and it won't move, just like some people. Plus, the heavy bag never lies. If you're off target, you'll know it. If you're too high or too low, you'll know it. (You'll probably fall down, which is how you'll know it.) To kick the heavy bag so that the blow is powerful enough to move *it* instead of *you*, you must hit it accurately, and you must hit it hard, transferring your energy to it. If you master this, you'll rarely find yourself bouncing off partners during sparring. (Of course, you would never kick your partner as hard as you kick the heavy bag!)

By following these techniques and modifying them to suit your needs, you can successfully spar taller, heavier opponents.

Kicking variety

Women who develop a strong repertoire of kicks have a significant advantage in sparring. Many kickboxers rely on just one or two kicks and make up the difference by punching. This can be a weakness. Since women generally have speed, flexibility and agility, you should be able to add almost any kick to your sparring arsenal. Use all the kicks you've learned. And use them in combinations. Remember to target different areas of the opponent's body: kick to the head with the roundhouse kick; kick to the body with the side kick or the front kick; kick to the thighs with the roundhouse kick. Use the turn back kick occasionally, just to surprise your opponent, especially if she has left her center line open during an attack.

By practicing these techniques, you'll become a better fighter—and, more importantly, you'll learn to enjoy fighting. Pretty soon, we won't be able to drag you out of the ring!

FOR WOMEN ONLY: It is extremely important to find the right coach if you're at all hesitant about sparring. If your coach refuses to allow you to grow comfortable with sparring by letting you do step sparring and no contact sparring, find another coach! A good coach will encourage you to move onto the next step when you're ready (and you may not think you are), but a good coach also recognizes that women have less experience with contact than men and should be willing to accommodate for that.

DEBZ SAYS: Remember, physical contact causes stimulation to the autonomic nervous system. Your first impulse is to stop what you're doing—to end whatever is causing the stimulation. To gain control over this "short circuit" effect from too much contact, practice taking volleys of hits from your partner. Gain control over your reaction to these bursts of contact, and when you get in the ring, you'll be able to withstand the physical contact with confidence.

19

FULL CONTACT SPARRING

Once you've mastered the basics of sparring, you're ready to hit and be hit. You're ready for full contact sparring. So you might expect this chapter to be about getting physically ready for that kind of sparring. But it's not. Well, OK, some of it is. This chapter focuses on your mental preparation, which plays a big role in your ability to succeed at sparring.

Goal setting

Goal setting is an excellent way to continually improve and achieve. For some people, the task of getting in shape, learning new skills and getting comfortable sparring can seem monumental. But, when the "task" is broken down to the smallest degree, it seems much more manageable.

If your goal is to become a champion kickboxer, and you've never even been to gym, you have some goal setting to do! First things first: start a journal and write in it faithfully. Start by defining your largest goal. Then decide how long it may take you to reach it—say, two years. Then, divide each year into quarters consisting of three months. Define goals which are cumulative for each quarter. Begin with the last quarter, the ultimate goal, first. Then determine the intermediate steps needed to get there. If your long term goal is, "I want to be a competitive kickboxer," then the quarterly goals might be:

Quarter 1: Begin strength training and cardio training to get in good physical condition. Begin altering diet for better athletic performance.

Quarter 2: On cardio training days, substitute a good cardio kickboxing class and begin learning basic kickboxing skills. Study films and instructional tapes on kickboxing and martial arts to assist in learning techniques.

Quarter 3: Become more advanced and intensify strength training methods. Check in with a nutritionist on diet to enhance training goals. Add bag work to kickboxing regimen. Begin relaxation, meditation or yoga training to aid in recovery of self-control.

Quarter 4: Begin attending competitions to see first hand what it's really like. Network with other fighters, coaches, managers and promoters. Take notes on questions you may have and slip these into your journal, along with inspirational photos of your mentors and heroes. Begin step sparring.

Quarter 5: Continually "up the ante" on intensifying training in all areas. Switch things up so the mind and body do not slip into a comfort zone. Begin light contact sparring. Ask for as much direction/constructive criticism as possible. Video tape your matches for further scrutiny and adjust your methodology accordingly. Set your sights on a competition you'd like to enter, perhaps within your own training group at first, and work each moment of training *knowing* you will win.

Quarter 6: Add full contact sparring. Make each round the "final" round. Fight like it's your last chance to win (or like your life or a loved one's life is endangered). See yourself attaining your goal.

Quarter 7: Check with nutritionist on adjusting diet and supplementation for optimum training now. You don't want this part of your program to hold you back. Also, it's of utmost importance to give yourself enough time for rest and recovery. Pay close attention now to your relaxation or meditation techniques. Use visualization and vivid imagery of yourself reaching your goal during this practice. Add plyometric training to fine tune athletic response.

Quarter 8: As the date for your competition draws near, train hard, stay focused, but do not overtrain! Double check your techniques, concentrating on weak areas and compensating for them. One week ahead of time, get more rest, eat well, and train for simple as well as complex situations.

As you can see, defining the quarters is one goal setting step, then breaking that down into smaller, more manageable steps, is another. Continue to break your goals down to the smallest degree, such as, "Today, I will perform all my basic kicks on the heavy bag 12 times each."

Mental preparation

In order to become the most accomplished kickboxer possible, keep an open mind. Watch other fighters and learn from them. Spar different partners and discuss your performance. Videotape your matches to see what tendencies crop up. Watch competitions to see what advanced fighters do. Read instructional articles and books and watch how-to videos. Most of all, practice on your own.

Much of sparring is mental preparation rather than physical exertion. If you have confidence, you're more likely to react quickly and without hesitation. If you're unsure, you may let opportunities to score pass you by. At first, it can be difficult to develop confidence, since you don't know what you're doing most of the time. That's why practicing timing techniques and combination drills is crucial. These drills help you spar with confidence.

Although you may get discouraged or frustrated when you spar, you must stay focused and continue to fight confidently. If you let your doubts influence you, your opponent will have won the match without scoring a point. Realize that even a bad sparring match helps you learn and grow.

To keep from getting distracted, concern yourself only with what you're doing. Are you taking advantage of openings that come up? Are you anticipating your opponent's attacks? Are you getting faster, stronger, smarter? Don't worry about how you compare to your opponent or to other kickboxers. Learn to be the best kickboxer you can be.

Size up your opponent

Analyze how you spar different fighters. Tall people, short people, heavy contact fighters, light contact fighters—all require a slightly different approach. If one opponent relies on a fast-paced, aggressive attack, your approach should be different from when you face a fighter who relies primarily on defensive countering techniques. Your opponents should not dictate the match, but you should respond to each individual as just that—an individual. If one person never gets out of the way of your front kick, by all means keep it coming. If another opponent easily evades it and counter-attacks successfully, find another approach. Sparring different people differently forces you to add variety to your sparring, which is essential to success in kickboxing.

Think of sparring as a work in progress, not a final product. It should change, grow, mature and adjust as you learn.

Gearing up for competition

Your everyday training in kickboxing is great for getting in shape and learning some self-defense moves. But to prepare to enter the ring as an amateur or a pro, you need to train specifically with that end in mind. You need a special workout and a plan.

Six to eight weeks ahead of time, you need to change your workout plan and your lifestyle. You need to start getting enough rest every night.

You have to drink tons of water every day. You need to make sure your diet is acceptable. Eating small meals throughout the day helps ensure that your body is adequately fueled all day long. A high-carbohydrate diet that's low in fat is best for preparing for a fight. You might also keep a journal detailing your preparations for the upcoming fight. This helps keep you focused on what you're aiming for. You should also check that your equipment is in good shape and that you have the right equipment for the fight. You should understand the rules ahead of time so that as you prepare, you take them into consideration. For example, if you're going to be fighting in three minute rounds, practicing in two minute rounds won't do you much good. This information should be obtained well ahead of time and should become part of your training plan.

During this period, you should visualize the fighter you'll be in the ring—a winner! Imagine how you'll evade attack and launch devastating kicks and punches. This helps you get mentally ready and counteracts all those butterflies in your stomach.

You should start training six days a week at this point. Alternate kickboxing days with weight training and cardio work. During the first week or so of training, work with your coach to determine your areas of weakness. Is your power lacking? Could you be a little more flexible? These will be shortcomings you'll address over the next month or two. Be sure your fighting is balanced between kicks and punches. Emphasizing one over the other will give your opponent an advantage.

Endurance is crucial to success in the ring, so even if you don't like aerobic training, you'll need to do some. The best kickboxers are also runners. You can also do treadmill and stairclimbing to improve your endurance.

You (or your manager) should investigate your competition so that you can make a plan. Is this a person with a lot of ring experience? Or is it someone who is just turning pro? Who is considered the contender? Map out a list of things you need to do to defeat your opponent. It may be that you just have to keep your hands up and go the full time. Or it might be that you have to avoid her high roundhouse kick, which means working on some ducking and slipping is in order.

Carefully break your goals down into the steps you need to succeed in the ring. If your roundhouse kick is not all it could be, determine how to correct that. Be specific about your goal. Write it down. "Create a faster, more powerful roundhouse kick," is a clear goal. But you still need to break this goal down into the steps you can take to create a faster, more powerful roundhouse kick. List the drills and exercises you can (and will) do to improve your kick. Leaf through this book to identify drills that will help, and talk with your coach to get his or her ideas. A vague sense that you need to "work on that" won't help much. A precise, clearly identified plan is the way to go.

Meticulous preparation and intense training will prepare you to enter the ring, fight your heart out and emerge victorious!

FOR WOMEN ONLY: Being the nurturing caretakers we are, women tend to do a lot of worrying. In kickboxing, this translates into, "Am I ready for this?" "What if I'm not ready for this?" "What if my opponent is ten times better than I am?" Instead of telling yourself not to worry, *answer the questions*. Are you ready for this? If you don't know, find out! Ask people you trust. Compare yourself to other competitors. What if you're not ready? You'll lose. Is that the worst thing in the world? No. And so on.

DEBZ SAYS: A good question to ask yourself periodically is, "*Why* am I doing this?" Remind yourself that you are just as important as everyone and everything else you, as a woman, must take care of. For some reason, we feel we must put ourselves and our priorities last on the list. Whether it's winning a kickboxing title or winning at life, you *must* put yourself first, and it's wise to remind yourself that this is a GOOD thing!

20
AVOIDING INJURY

Although training in kickboxing can lead to injury, it isn't inevitable. Taking sensible precautions can prevent some of the most common injuries. For instance, warming up and stretching before a vigorous workout, and cooling down and stretching even more afterward, can prevent common strains and sprains.

Because women are more prone to certain injuries than men, they should pay particular attention to preventing these injuries. Women have knee and hip injuries more frequently than men (while men have more trouble with hamstring and groin pulls). Overall, the most common injuries in kickboxing are overuse injuries, hyperextension injuries, sprains, strains, bruises and lacerations.

To prevent knee and hip injuries, women should pay particular attention to strengthening the muscles around these joints and in stabilizing the joints. This means building up the quadriceps and hamstrings to minimize problems with knees. Building strong abs and adductors and abductors (thigh muscles) will help strengthen your back and hips.

Also crucial to preventing injury is performing techniques correctly. If you don't pivot when you do a side kick, for instance, you put excessive stress on your knee, twisting it in a damaging way. Be scrupulous about practicing techniques correctly. No technique should put undue stress on a joint. If it does, you're probably doing the technique incorrectly. Ask your coach or trainer for advice on performing techniques correctly, building strength and stabilizing joints.

It should go without saying that you should always seek medical advice for any injury or unexplained swelling, tenderness or pain.

Overuse injuries

Overuse injuries occur when a joint is used repetitively, especially when the joint is not accustomed to the use.

158

Tendinitis and bursitis

The two most common overuse injuries, teninitis and bursitis, can cause pain and discomfort in a joint when an individual begins using the joint more than usual. To prevent this problem, stretch before working out and execute techniques precisely. On a turning kick, such as a roundhouse kick, if you don't pivot correctly, you'll put undue stress on your hips and knees, which can cause overuse injuries and other damage.

Although painful and frustrating, overuse injuries rarely cause more than temporary discomfort. If you suspect you have an overuse injury, check with your physician. Visiting with a sports medicine specialist or even a sports trainer can help you to learn how to prevent such problems.

Usually rest, ice, and an anti-inflammatory such as ibuprofen (or in more extreme cases, a prescription medication) will ease the problem. If not, your doctor may recommend an injection of cortisone and/or physical therapy treatment.

While overuse injuries can affect all joints, for women hips and knees are most commonly overused, followed by the shoulders. Most women don't have the same amount of upper body strength as their male counterparts. Since kickboxing requires using a lot of punches, your shoulders undergo more stress and strain than usual. Since the muscle mass is usually not as well-developed here as in other parts of the body, these stresses and strains are more likely to cause an injury. Remember to stretch all of your joints before you start training and to perform techniques exactly as described. Also, try not to temper your gung-ho attitude until your body is ready for it. Start your training slowly, building up your intensity and tempo over time.

Stress fractures

Stress fractures usually occur over a period of time. A bone that must withstand repeated blows may develop a break or a series of small fissures that have the effect of a fracture. In kickboxing these kinds of fractures occasionally occur, usually in a foot or hand. Using proper technique and limiting the amount of abuse you direct toward any one area of your body can help prevent such an injury. A stress fracture can feel similar to a broken bone, or it can feel like an overuse injury.

Hyperextension injuries

Hyperextension occurs when a joint moves beyond its usual stopping point. This can happen when you throw a punch or kick with full energy but no target absorbs the energy of the strike. Kicking the heavy bag will rarely cause a hyperextension injury because the heavy bag absorbs the energy and power of the kick. But when you kick air (as you might do when practicing in training class or in front of a mirror), your energy isn't absorbed and your momentum isn't stopped. Therefore, your arm or leg can move beyond its normal range and hyperextend a joint.

To prevent hyperextension, always keep your joints slightly bent. Never fully extend and lock out a knee or elbow joint.

You can easily identify hyperextension. Sudden pain in a joint after you execute a technique or pain that persists whenever you use the affected limb indicates a possible hyperextension. Rest, ice, anti-inflammatories—and, if pain continues or worsens—a visit to the doctor are all called for.

Acute Injuries

Strains, sprains, tears, cuts and bruises result from an acute injury—that is, a single event that happens suddenly and causes an injury. Perhaps you roll your wrist when your punch lands and end up with a sprain. Of course, in the sparring ring, you're going to get hit occasionally, and you might end up with a big bruise.

Sprains and strains can range from mild to severe. The milder cases require little attention, perhaps some aspirin and some ice. More serious cases require rest, ice, compression and elevation, a treatment also known by its acronym "RICE."

Strain

The usual signs of a strain include pain, tenderness and swelling. If the muscle doesn't seem to work at all, seek treatment immediately. Surgery may be necessary to repair the damage.

A muscle strain happens when you overstretch a muscle. The word "pull" is often used to describe a strain. The muscle continues to function—it just becomes sore. More serious strains may result in muscle tears, which require more time and rest to heal. In kickboxing, the most common strains occur in the hamstring and the groin area. For women, the hip flexor (the small muscles running from the hip to the top of the thigh) are commonly affected. Most strains are quick to mend. Put ice on the area intermittently for 24 hours. After a day, you can use a heating pad. A few days of rest are usually sufficient for healing.

To prevent strains, warm up and stretch before working out. Building muscle and increasing your flexibility will reduce your chances of straining your muscles.

Sprain

A sprain occurs when the ligaments that connect muscles to bones are injured. Usually a twist, a misstep or an extreme stretch puts too much strain on the ligaments, and tissue is torn. Sprains commonly happen to the ankles and knees. Signs include rapid swelling, reduced ability to use the affected area and pain. If you actually hear a snapping sound, seek treatment immediately. You may have a detached ligament. Surgery is sometimes needed to repair the damage.

For routine sprains, ice, compression and rest will cure the condition. The sprained part can usually bear weight after a day or too, but remember this doesn't mean it is completely healed. For a few weeks, minimize your workout intensity to avoid worsening the sprain. If the sprain is severe or the joint is unstable, the area may need to be immobilized with a cast or splint. If you repeatedly strain or sprain a certain part of your body, use a brace, wrap or tape to help support the area and prevent progressive damage to the area. Consult your physician, who can recommend a sports trainer or a physical therapist for tips on preventing recurring injuries.

Cuts and bruises

Bruises and cuts are probably the most common kickboxing injuries. Usually, some ice or a bandage will suffice. For more serious cases, you may need to visit the doctor. Bleeding that won't stop is a sign to seek medical help.

Rest, ice, compression, and elevation can help bruises heal. See a doctor if the injury doesn't improve or if there's the possibility of a fracture. Use sparring equipment (shin pads, chest protectors, etc.) to reduce cuts and bruises.

Fractures

Fractures aren't always obvious. Pain, loss of function, and swelling indicate the possibility of a fracture, but the symptoms sometimes resemble the symptoms of a sprain. X-rays may be needed to determine the extent of an injury. Some fractures, such as with the small bones of the feet or hands, cannot be treated very well, except by resting the affected area. Sometimes you can tape the injured finger or toe to the one next to it to provide additional support and prevent further trauma.

Fractures heal slowly, over weeks or even months. Usually, the broken bone must be kept immobile through the use of a cast or splint. Sometimes screws or a plate must be attached to help the bone heal. A fractured bone may require physical therapy treatment. Otherwise, muscle tone is lost, stiffness occurs and healing is slower.

Dislocations

Dislocations happen after an acute injury. A dislocation occurs when the ends of the bones of the joint slip out of their normal position, causing pain, swelling and difficulty using the affected joint. Sometimes a dislocation will injure nearby muscles and ligaments. Seek treatment immediately to distinguish a dislocation from a fracture, to determine the extent of damage, and to prevent further damage to the surrounding tissues. Usually the dislocation is easily corrected and the area is immobilized for a few days.

Do not resume full speed training until your physician has cleared it. You can reinjure the joint, and even cause permanent damage and disability. Physical therapy may also help strengthen the surrounding muscles and ligaments to prevent a recurrence of a dislocation.

Back injuries

Injuries and strains to the back should always be treated with care because of the possible involvement of the spinal column. Spinal cord injuries are rare, but the possibility exists. Any sharp pain in the back should be treated. Unexplained tenderness or swelling may be signs of concern and should be checked out as well.

A note of caution: if you're taking painkillers or other medications (over the counter or prescription), make sure you know how your body handles it before you start working out. Some medications cause nausea and vomiting (not ideal when you're working out vigorously); others cause dizziness, which could interfere with your balance (not a good problem for a kickboxer to have) and still others make you tired and sluggish (not the best condition to spar in). Ask your doctor or pharmacist about side effects to be aware of.

Although it is not uncommon to have a kickboxing-related injury, such injuries can often be prevented if you use your common sense. Any fitness program should include a warm-up, stretching, the exercise itself, and a cool down period that also includes stretching. In some kickboxing classes, you'll be responsible for your own warming up, stretching and cooling down. Don't try to save time by skipping these essential steps. Instead, make them part of your workout and help prevent injuries.

FOR WOMEN ONLY: When women get excited about kickboxing, they often express their enthusiasm by training every day of the week even if their previous exercise consisted of getting off the sofa to see what was in the refrigerator. This is a prime cause of overuse injuries. Even if you're motivated about training, pace yourself in the beginning. Attend training two or three times a week. If you really feel the need to do more training at first, alternate your workouts so that sometimes you're doing cardiowork and sometimes you're kickboxing. This reduces the amount of stress on your joints until you can strengthen them and avoid overuse injuries.

DEBZ SAYS: It's important to note a particular problem for women: softening of ligaments and loosening of joints caused by hormonal changes. It was previously thought that this occurred only during pregnancy, but recent studies show that this condition also occurs to a lesser degree during the premenstrual phase of a woman's monthly cycle. Softer ligaments and looser joints can easily lead to injury if one isn't careful. It's imperative that female athletes take more care to warm up and stretch during this time to avoid injury. If you notice a trend toward minor (or major) injuries during the premenstrual phase (or while pregnant) you may wish to scale back your training intensity at this time.

21
OTHER PRACTICAL MATTERS

Women who have been physically active most of their lives, participating in sports from the time they were old enough to throw a ball, have developed methods for handling the practical concerns of female athletes. But many women have never participated in sports before acquiring an interest in kickboxing, or they haven't played sports or worked out much as adults although they might have as children. For these women, advice from the experienced can help.

Menstruation and stress incontinence

For those of us who menstruate or have stress incontinence (perhaps from child-bearing), simple problems occur. With all that kicking and stretching, it is easy to leak. Sometimes women avoid training during their period because of this concern, but that's not a good solution at all. First, remind yourself that no one cares. Adults should be able to handle it, kids ignore it, only you are worried about it.

Some women will use two forms of protection to help prevent leaks. Some wear disposable absorbent undergarments. These work well for women whose menstrual periods are heavy. Disposable undergarments are, indeed, cumbersome, and may restrict movement slightly. Biker shorts, made from stretchable, form-fitting material, can be worn under your workout clothes to help keep leaks from showing. You can find biker shorts in the women's athletic wear department of most bigger clothing stores.

Since the menstrual cycle occasionally causes bloating and tenderness, you may want to keep a looser fitting workout outfit around for those days. You may feel tired, sluggish and weak. While this can't be overcome, instead of becoming frustrated, redirect your kickboxing goals. Work on stretching more during those times when you feel as if your speed is lacking. Practice technique if you can't bear the thought of bag kicking.

If necessary, take pain relievers to help with cramps, and drink plenty of water before class. You'll probably become fatigued more quickly and easily than usual because you have less blood and less iron in your blood than usual. Your doctor can advise you on using supplemental iron tablets. Higher protein intake during this phase will help alleviate mood swings, head and body aches, and cravings for sweets.

You will also need to take special care *before* your period. Recent studies have shown that hormonal changes that occur during a woman's premenstrual phase can soften ligaments and loosen joints, which could cause injury. Pay attention to your body and respond to its needs. Keep a journal and record your experiences; if you detect a trend—for instance, you get more strains and sprains the week before your period—you can more easily do something about it than if you only have a vague idea that some times you're more prone to injury than other times.

Menopause

In menopause, your hormone levels vary, so your energy level varies. You may be more sensitive to climate and suffer hot flashes and experience headaches. Exercise can help ease these conditions. It also helps maintain strong bones and muscles. Incorporating soy isoflavonens as a protein source has produced good results in most women experiencing hot flashes and mood swings. This product can be found in most health food or supplement shops.

You may be more prone to injury during and after menopause than you were before. Thus, it is especially important to take steps to prevent injury. In addition, good stretching can help you maintain flexibility, which many women complain is their first physical ability to go. Continuing kickboxing—even starting kickboxing—will keep you strong and flexible physically and mentally throughout the rest of your life.

Pregnancy

Female kickboxers often wonder what happens when they become pregnant. What will they do now? Obviously, they're going to shelve their plans for a pro kickboxing debut for at least a couple of months. The good news is that pregnant women who exercised regularly before pregnancy can continue to do so during and after pregnancy, though you must remember to keep your workouts reasonable. Exercise can help you have an easier labor, faster recovery, and more stamina after delivery.

Pregnancy is *not* the time start training in kickboxing. Even if you've been working out regularly, check with your doctor before continuing to work out.

As your pregnancy progresses, you'll have to modify what you can do. Don't get discouraged by this. Above all, don't quit! Just slow down a bit. Remember that because of changes in your body, you're more easily injured during pregnancy than at any other time. Your weight distribution and center of gravity shift, making you more likely to lose your balance and fall.

Avoid exercises that require you to lie on your back. This could restrict blood flow to the fetus. You may become tired faster than usual, and you should listen to your body. Now is not the time to push it. Drink plenty of fluids and avoid working out when it's extremely hot and humid.

Stop sparring as soon as you find out you're pregnant. You should also perform other techniques with no contact in order to prevent accidental blows to your abdomen. Although your body will protect your baby quite well, it makes sense not to take unnecessary risks.

Modify your practice as needed. You can still focus on the fundamentals, which will help you remain sharp and focused. Listen to your body, don't push, and you can continue working toward your kickboxing goals even when you're nine months along.

After childbirth

Your recovery period after childbirth may be only a few weeks, but in the case of a very difficult delivery or a C-section, it may be six or eight weeks before your doctor clears you to return to working out. During this period, think about your training even though you can't work out. Take the time to read all those how-to books while nursing the baby, watch films, go and view class, then show baby off to your fellow students and instructors.

As your doctor allows you, add in some light exercise, such as stretching. You can do this while your baby naps. Walk instead of parking the car near the front door of the grocery store. Do more lifting and carrying as you get closer to full strength.

Read up on kickboxing as you recover. Learn about different kinds of martial arts—you may be able to use something that you learn. Watch videos during those times when you'd normally work out. Examine what they do, how they do it, and why they do it.

As you ease your way back to a full workout, don't worry if you're not up to full speed right away. Take your time, go slow, and you'll get back on track.

Preparing for the everyday workout

Many women learn, through trial and error, what they need to do to prepare for working out. But women agree on some basic tips. Don't eat just before you workout. The digestive process will make you sluggish. But an empty stomach won't fuel your workout, so eat a small snack, nothing more substantial than an apple, about an hour before you plan to work out. A few ounces of juice can also fuel your workout without making you sluggish. Drink several glasses of water to fill up on fluids during the hour before your workout. Stop the liquids about 20 minutes before class. Drinking at least 16 ounces and preferably 24 ounces of water before working out will keep your stomach full, without diverting energy to digestion. This will help you to feel less tired and more energetic.

Equipping for class

One of the first things you'll discover is that everything from bag gloves uniform to headgear is made to fit men. This doesn't mean that there aren't good pieces of equipment for women—just that they aren't obvious. It requires some patience to find the things you need.

Unless otherwise specified, all equipment and uniforms are in men's sizes. This means that for women, regardless of the size they order, the equipment will fit strangely. A few manufacturers are starting to design equipment just for women. See Chapter 22 for further information.

Don't wear makeup. It runs, smears on the uniform, and gets in your eyes. Trim your nails—fingernails and toenails both. Artificial nails of any kind can be dangerous, especially if they catch on loose clothing. Also, long fingernails can be dangerous to your partners.

If your hair gets in the way as you practice, consider a shorter cut or keep it pulled back. If you don't want to pull it back in a pony tail because that causes breakage, consider a loose braid. This keeps hair out of your face, and since it is loosely braided, causes less damage to your hair. To keep sweat out of your eyes—and if you have lots of hair, your scalp will sweat more—tie a rolled-up bandanna around your forehead. This absorbs perspiration, looks OK (kickboxers get to wear headbands if they want) and also helps to keep your hair out of your eyes.

For sparring equipment, keep in mind that men's sizes are about one size larger than women's. Small gloves will fit a woman with medium-sized hands. For shin and footguards, usually sold in small, medium and large sizes, it's helpful to know that a small fits a woman's foot size 6 to 7. Medium fits 8 and 9. Large fits size 10 and above. If you wear a smaller size than a 6, and an extra small is not available, try children's shoe sizes.

Martial arts shoes and sometimes shin and footguards are often sold in regular men's sizes. Men's 3–13 is the usual range. Men's shoes are about a size and a half larger than women's. A woman who wears a size 9 show will probably be comfortable in a men's size 7 ½ or 8. Again, foot width as well as length and personal comfort will affect the actual size that works best, but these measurements should give you an idea of where to begin.

Role model

One of the consequences of the gender-related stereotypes we all suffer from is that you'll be the standard by which other women are judged—which can be a bit of a burden, if you think about it. As a female kickboxer, it's important to be a good role model for other women and girls, too.

For this reason, you'll have to develop even more perseverance and self-control than male kickboxers do. But it will be worth it in the long run. Take the time to show new female kickboxers the ropes. Give them the benefit of your insights.

Developing physical confidence

Developing the confidence to kick and punch hard—and without inhibition—can be fun and rewarding. Doing techniques well requires the right speed, timing and power—none of which you'll have if you're tentative or unsure. Make a commitment to the technique—even if you do end up executing it incorrectly. Any instructor would rather see an incorrectly performed low roundhouse kick done with enthusiasm than a perfectly done low roundhouse kick performed slowly with little confidence. Even if the enthusiastic low kick isn't perfect, it has a much better chance of being successful and doing what it is supposed to do (i.e., attack the low section) than a kick correctly done with little interest or effort.

Often, we are told to practice perfectly. What this means is that we should pay attention to each kick and punch and try to perform it the best way we know how. Because you want to reach perfection even in practice, you should be unwilling to settle for what is simply comfortable. It isn't practice that makes perfect, but perfect practice that makes perfect, as so many sports philosophers have pointed out. But unless you're constantly attempting to outdo and challenge yourself, you aren't practicing perfectly. And this means occasionally you will fall down or look stupid or stand there and get hit when you could have moved out of the way. This is all part of the learning process.

Women, especially those who have not been athletic in the past, do bring more self-consciousness to kickboxing than men do. They're much harder on themselves than men are, wanting to do things correctly, right away, immediately. This can be frustrating. It can also be discouraging.

Kickboxing can help you become stronger, braver, more fit, more flexible and stress free. This only works when you release your self-criticism and enjoy what you can do and what you do well. This doesn't mean we should not be critical for ourselves or that we don't need to strive for improvement. It simply means we should give ourselves a chance and not write ourselves off too early in the game.

What to do about other people

Women in kickboxing occasionally encounter others (often men, but not always) who have a condescending or belittling attitude toward them. Because the instructor sets the tone for the gym and is ultimately responsible for all that happens there, if he or she is setting a good example, then such attitudes will be discouraged. If you occasionally work with a person who has a cocky attitude, that's just a minor headache, comparable to many minor headaches we deal with each day. Some people refuse to co-operate appropriately. This is especially intimidating if you're at a stage where you need encouragement. Some people may even belittle your efforts, or simply stand there and sigh while holding a target that you're attempting to hit. If the person might actually have some useful advice for you or some relevant feedback, try asking for it. If a person is actively involved in your success or failure, he or she will often display a better, more team-oriented attitude. Sometimes ignoring the behavior and showing it doesn't affect you, makes it disappear. Sometimes it doesn't matter much what you do, you still find yourself in an occasional unpleasant encounter. One of the most important things you can do to minimize the effect such encounters have on you and training is to develop a support network of other kickboxers, especially other female kickboxers. It is important to have the encouragement and support of others as you pursue your training. Talking, even just in the locker room after class, can help you feel less alone.

Women who have been in your situation often have useful advice. Also, if a particular student tends to belittle you, he or she probably belittles other students as well, and they may have found a successful way of dealing with him. This is true of many situations you may discover in the course of your training. Not only can you gain insight, but you'll have people cheering you on and supplying the necessary encouragement to succeed.

As you continue to train, you will get to know the people you train with better. This helps you to develop strategies for dealing with them. It also helps them to get to know you, and see you as a person, someone who is similar to them. Often this helps them realize their behavior is inappropriate. Thus, patience, tough as it is, is sometimes your only refuge for dealing with negative attitudes.

Sometimes, however, the situation is a little more serious than lack of encouragement. There are, unfortunately, a number of men (and some women) who think they have something to prove to women, such as they have more testosterone. The delightful thing is when you are better than such men and you can beat them in a sparring match. However, especially when you're first beginning your training, such people are sometimes superior in skill, though not in personality, and you can't beat them. Sometimes these people can be dangerous, because instead of being passively negative, they're actively negative. Perhaps they spar too hard, or they lack control when they kick. If this happens, you must immediately speak up and explain that they're being too aggressive and could injure you. In such extreme cases, you should discuss the problem with the instructor. Among other things, the instructor needs to be aware of such a potential liability, for someone who is overly aggressive with one person is probably overly aggressive with many people. In the worst case, you should refuse to work with a person who lacks proper control and could injure you. This, of course, happens only rarely, and you will probably never encounter a person whose attitude is actually dangerous to you.

Gender differences

More common is that attitude that is unpleasant because it focuses unnecessary attention on your gender. Many otherwise extremely nice men are burdened with this problem. Perhaps you're sparring with a male partner, and he kicks or punches to your chest, accidentally touching your breast. Some men stop the match and grovel abjectly for forgiveness, which is just plain embarrassing for both people involved. If the chest is a target area, of course you're occasionally going to hit a woman's breast. That's simply how it is, but it's very embarrassing for some men, and they can make it embarrassing for you, too. With experience, such men quit being embarrassed, so usually your best bet is to ignore it, which also means not drawing attention to any such situations. You might say "no problem" to acknowledge an apology, but don't let it sidetrack you. Sometimes joking can ease the situation, because you acknowledge their embarrassment but also put the incident in its proper perspective. This sort of attention to your gender is more understandable and more forgivable than other kinds of negative attention. Such men are genuinely concerned that they might have hurt you or embarrassed you, so a quick reassurance that this is not the case can help them understand that you aren't the fragile, breakable type.

Sometimes such men, overly concerned with the fact that you're a woman, attempt to encourage or compliment you by saying you're as good as a man. Such comments can be annoying, to say the least, but usually they're meant in a good way. Such men and such comments are just a little misguided. Usually a "thanks," is good enough, although some women have occasionally been provoked to respond, "and you're as quick as a woman," or "you're as flexible as a child," to help them understand that such comments are not necessarily the best praise. Though we prefer to be judged on our performance, not our gender, such attitudes are easier to handle than are the more misogynistic attitudes.

Unwanted advances

On occasion, kickboxers training together enjoy each other's company outside the ring. In one gym, three couples have met and married in the last few years. Obviously, men and women can be attracted to each other even with sweat dripping down their faces. While mutually acceptable relationships can form, as in any mixed gender situation, the occasional unwanted advance may come along. It often comes as a surprise to women that they have to deal with unwanted interest in the gym.

If someone makes unwanted advances, and you've turned him down, and he persists, the same rules apply as in other situations. You can complain to the instructor, you can talk firmly to the offending individual again, you can ask the instructor not to pair you with him in class, you can avoid him by attending different classes from the ones he attends. The least disruptive method, though, is probably to interact with others before and after class, so that he will have less opportunity to bother you. Grab a partner and do partner stretches, for instance. Work on a technique with another person. Ignore him while working on improving your skills. This will, in the end, discourage most men. While it is frustrating to encounter unwanted interest in what you might hope to be a neutral environment, annoying persistence is comparatively rare and can usually be managed.

A note of caution: getting involved with your trainer or instructor is not always a good idea. If you're trying to succeed as a kickboxer, you want a coach who'll train you hard without regard to the fact that you have a date tonight. If the relationship breaks up, unpleasant side effects can happen. Some women report that after a break up, their instructors have tried to embarrass or humiliate them in class, while another woman reports that she was actually barred from attending classes after she broke up with her coach. As in an employee-employer situation, think twice before getting involved with someone who has power over you and your kickboxing goals.

Misconceptions

For the most part, your kickboxing experience will be rewarding, but if and when you run into sexist attitudes, try not to let them discourage you. Negativity toward female kickboxers is usually the result of misconceptions that men have. Though it is not your responsibility to educate them, unless you want to, an understanding of these misconceptions can help you remain patient. Be aware, however, that in some gyms it is acceptable to buy into these misconceptions, to consider women less talented or less important than men. It is imperative to steer clear of such places. If you're in one now, get out! Rest assured that most instructors, however, discourage unfair or unequal treatment of women, and it is just a few individual people who may cause you distress.

Misconceptions about female kickboxers abound. Non-kickboxers think they're unusual, unfeminine and otherwise different from "normal" women. Male kickboxers may believe they're not as dedicated, not as talented, not as serious and not as strong. But of course all people are dedicated, talented, serious and strong to varying degrees having nothing to do with gender.

The right attitude

The key to successful training in kickboxing is to not concern yourself with other people's reactions to you. Ultimately, you are simply responsible for you. You must focus on giving it your best effort. The less attention you pay to other people's negative attitudes, the less likely such attitudes will affect you, and the less likely such attitudes toward you will continue. Negative behavior or attitudes tend to disappear as you gain more self-confidence. Kickboxing can, after all, be a humbling experience. Everyone makes stupid mistakes sometimes and everyone finds one opponent who is impossible to fight, and everyone falls down while performing a high roundhouse kick at least now and then. A good sense of humor is an asset and a valuable training tool!

Balancing kickboxing and family life

Sometimes family members will have difficulty dealing with how much time you spend away, practicing kickboxing. Friends, children, spouses and parents all can make it difficult if they don't support you. After all, it takes more time and money to participate in the kickboxing than not to participate.

If those around you are not supportive, the best approach to take is to try to educate them. Explain what you're doing and have them visit a class. Let your coach tell them about your progress. You may want to describe the benefits you receive from your practice. It might make you feel more fit and healthier. Or maybe it helps you feel less stressed. It might give you self-confidence or help you lose weight. Make it clear that these benefits are important to you.

Setting a schedule and sticking with it helps take some of the pressure off you and your family. If everyone knows that Tuesday and Thursday nights are always kickboxing nights, they can adjust more easily than if sometimes you're gone on Mondays and Thursdays and sometimes on Tuesdays, Fridays and Saturday mornings, or what have you. Setting a schedule helps others cooperate as well. If your husband knows you always work out on Mondays and Wednesdays, and that it's his job to feed the kids, chances are the entire operation will run more smoothly than if no one, including you, knows when you plan to practice this week.

For your family, more drastic measures may have to be taken. You may need—or simply want—to get them involved. Just as having a workout partner helps you go to the gym three times a week, having another member of your family practicing kickboxing with you can help you both stay motivated, even during those times when you're frustrated with your progress. Spouses who work out together can encourage each other and support each other; your spouse can at least give it a try to find out why you devote time and money to it. Children, if they are old enough, are also often interested in kickboxing. You may wish to sign them up for a few lessons. If they're involved, too, they'll be much more tolerant of the time you spend training. Just as spouses who work out together stay involved in kickboxing longer, so too do families who work out together.

For other people, friends are not supportive. This is more commonly a frustration among young, single people who rely on their friends for approval and encouragement. Often, their misconceptions are at the root of any teasing or lack of understanding that you may encounter. When this is the case, providing further information can help. Good friends will eventually understand. This doesn't mean that the friends who continue to tease you should immediately be dumped and never spoken to again, but you will have to refrain from talking about kickboxing around them. This means you'll avoid giving them the opportunity to make comments or sarcastic remarks. If they still do so, ignore the comments. Often, friends also just need to be told about the benefits of kickboxing—things like self-discipline, fitness and so on. Letting your friends in on your doubts and insecurities as well as your triumphs and rewards helps them put the whole adventure into perspective and might even motivate them to participate as well.

But whether your friends and family support you or not, and regardless of any attitudes you might encounter in the gym, it is the matter of your own attitude that counts most. With the right attitude, you can become a better kickboxer than you ever imagined. Keep positive and stay focused on your own goals. Don't let others dissuade you. You may never win fame and glory, but you will win self-confidence and self-esteem, you'll become more fit and less stressed, and you'll learn that you're capable of far more than you ever believed possible.

FOR WOMEN ONLY: Choose a female-friendly gym. Make sure at least some of the kickboxing students are women, and watch how the instructor interacts with any female students. Also look at the level of competence in the female students. Do they seem to know what they're doing? If so, someone helped them get there. Find out who that person is. Some women thrive with female instructors, so if this is you, find a gym that has at least one on staff.

FOR WOMEN ONLY: Finding a mentor can be important for you to succeed. A good mentor is one that helps you make progress toward your goals, helps you define those goals, and encourages you to get back on track if you derail. A mentor doesn't have to be a women to understand a woman's needs, but sometimes it helps. Women who've been there, done that can often offer insight. Once you've reached a level of competence in kickboxing, you too should think about becoming a mentor. You don't have to mentor only women, but remember to give a helping hand to the people who come to the sport after you do.

DEBZ SAYS: Kickboxing is as much a mental activity as a physical one. Use your head and don't forget to extend your inner power when dealing with negative people and unsupportive friends. Take a winning attitude into all areas of your life, not just the ring!

22
RESOURCES

Clothing and equipment

Call or write the following martial arts/kickboxing supply companies (some have websites). They carry clothing and equipment for women:

- Ringside, Inc. 9650 Dice Lane, Lenexa, Kansas 66215. (877) 4-Boxing. www.ringside.com.
- Fairtex. Muay Thai equipment. 2995 Junipero Serra Blvd., Daly City, CA 94014. (888) 512-7727. Fax: (650) 994-9021. www.fairtex.com
- Everlast. Sporting goods, including boxing and kickboxing equipment. Can be found in retail stores. 1350 Broadway, #2300, New York, NY 10018. www.everlast.com.
- Title Sports. Sporting goods, including boxing and kickboxing equipment. 14371 West 100th Street, Building C, Lenexa, KS 66215. (800) 999-1213. Fax: (913) 492-7546. www.titlesports.com.
- Turtle Shells. Protective sports bras and chest protectors for women. P.O. Box 5266, Edmonton, OK 73083. (800) 999-0927. www.turtle-shells.com.
- Bu Jin Design. Clothing and equipment designed especially for women. (866) 444-3644. Fax: (303) 444-1137. www.bujindesign.com
- Century Martial Art Supply. 1705 National Blvd, Midwest City, OK 73110-7942. (405) 732-2226. www.centuryma.com.
- Kwon, Inc. 3755 Broadmoor, SE, Grand Rapids, MI 49512. www.kwon.com
- Asian World of Martial Arts. 11601 Caroline Road, Philadelphia, PA 19154-2177. (800) 345-2962. www.awma.com.
- Macho Products, Inc. 10045 102nd Terrace, Sebastien, FL 32958. (800) 327-6812. www.macho.com.
- The Dragon's Choice. 8028 H Street, Omaha, NE 68127. (402) 651-3608. www.the dragonschoice.com.

- Pil Sung Martial Art Supply. 6300 Ridglea Place, Suite 1008, Fort Worth, TX 76116. (817) 738-5408. www.pil-sung.com
- Health in Balance. Supplies especially for women. 647 Hillsborough Street, Oakland, CA 94606. (510) 452-2990. www.home.earthlink.net/~healthbalanc/

Ask your instructor for any catalogs he or she may have; many supply houses, have women's stuff in stock.

Organizations and associations

If you have internet access, you can check out a number of websites with chat rooms, message boards, articles, directories and the like. Start with www.kickboxing.com and www.worldkickboxing.com.

- International Kickboxing Federation. P.O. Box 1205, Newcastle, CA 95658. www.ikfkickboxing.com.
- International Sport Karate Association. P.O. Box 90147, Gainesville, FL 32607-0147. (352) 374-6876. Fax: (352) 378-4454. www.iska.com.
- National Association of Professional Martial Artists. 5601 116th Avenue North, Clearwater, FL 33760. (800) 973-6734. www.napma.com.
- The National Women's Martial Arts Federation can help you feel less isolated. They hold training camps and seminars. P.O. Box 44433, Detroit, MI 48244-0433. www.nwmaf.org.
- Association of Women Martial Arts Instructors. P.O. Box 7033, Houston, TX 77248. http://members.aol.com/AWMAI/home.html.

INDEX